# Race, Gender, and the
# Politics of Skin Tone

# Race, Gender, and the Politics of Skin Tone

## Margaret L. Hunter

Routledge
Taylor & Francis Group

NEW YORK AND LONDON

Published in 2005 by
Routledge
Taylor & Francis Group
270 Madison Avenue
New York, NY 10016

Published in Great Britain by
Routledge
Taylor & Francis Group
2 Park Square
Milton Park, Abingdon
Oxon OX14 4RN

Printed in the United States of America on acid-free paper
10 9 8 7 6 5 4 3 2 1

International Standard Book Number-10: 0-415-94607-7 (Hardcover) 0-415-94608-5 (Softcover)
International Standard Book Number-13: 978-0-415-94607-0 (Hardcover) 978-0-415-94608-7 (Softcover)

### Library of Congress Cataloging-in-Publication Data

Hunter, Margaret L., 1972-
    Race, gender, and the politics of skin tone / Margaret L. Hunter.
        p. cm.
    Includes bibliographical references and index.
    ISBN 0-415-94607-7 (alk. paper) -- ISBN 0-415-94608-5 (pbk. : alk. paper)
    1. African Americans--Race identity. 2. Mexican Americans--Race identity. 3. African American women--Social conditions. 4. Mexican American women--Social conditions. 5. Interviews--United States. 6. Human skin color--United States--Psychological aspects. 7. Human skin color--Social aspects--United States. 8. Racism--United States. 9. United States--Race relations. I. Title.

E185.625.H865 2005
305.48'896073--dc22                                                                  2004029634

Taylor & Francis Group
is the Academic Division of T&F Informa plc.

Visit the Taylor & Francis Web site at
http://www.taylorandfrancis.com

and the Routledge Web site at
http://www.routledge-ny.com

To my parents

# CONTENTS

# ACKNOWLEDGMENTS

I am deeply indebted to Walter Allen, Vilma Ortiz, Sandra Harding, and Laura Miller for their input into this project over the years. I want to especially thank Sandra Harding for all of her help securing a contract for this book. I am forever indebted to Walter Allen, my advisor, mentor, and friend for all of his guidance, both intellectual and personal, throughout the past decade. Cedric Herring and Verna Keith gave me early encouragement in this area of study and continue to challenge my thinking and writing in this area. The editorial staff at Routledge provided lots of enthusiasm and support for this project. James Jackson, principal investigator for the National Survey of Black Americans and Carlos Arce, principal investigator for the National Chicano Survey made access to the data sets possible. The many women I interviewed for this project were open and forthright in our conversations. Their honesty is what makes this book compelling.

My parents taught me to be curious about our world, to ask questions, and to make changes. They have also been my biggest cheerleaders along the way. Thanks are not enough for my husband, Zeus, who engaged in countless conversations about the politics of race and provided enormous encouragement in finishing the book. And a special thanks belongs to Max, who allowed me to finish this manuscript during his naps.

# 1

## COLORSTRUCK

If you're white you're alright, if you're brown stick around, if you're yellow you're mellow, if you're black get back! Light, bright, and almost white. Blue-black. African. La güera. La prieta. La morena. India. La negrita. Colorstruck.

The blacker the berry, the sweeter the juice. This saying, unlike many others, promises an even sweeter inside for a person with dark brown skin and suggests that darker skin is actually more desirable than light. This book investigates the nature of skin tone in the African American[1] and Mexican American[2] communities and uncovers the hidden benefits and penalties for both light and dark skin. Ultimately, this book will assess whether the sentiment of the blacker the berry is illusion or reality.

Most Americans are familiar with problems of racial discrimination in the United States. African Americans and Mexican Americans have made great progress in combating persistent racial discrimination whether encountered in housing, education, the work place, or other areas. Hidden within the process of racial discrimination, is the often overlooked issue of colorism. Lighter-skinned African Americans and Mexican Americans enjoy substantial privileges that are still unattainable to their darker-skinned brothers and sisters.[3] Colorism is a problem affecting all Americans. Although typically described as a "black" or "Chicano" problem, colorism is practiced by whites and people of color alike. Given the opportunity, many people will hire a light-skinned person before a dark-skinned person of the same race, or choose to marry a lighter-skinned woman rather than a darker-skinned woman.[4]

1

Even the federal government is becoming increasingly concerned with color-based discrimination. "The Equal Employment Opportunity Commission [EEOC]...says it is handling more color-discrimination complaints pitting blacks, Hispanics, Native Americans, and others against members of their own race or ethnic group."[5] In the early 1990s, the EEOC typically received less than 500 complaints of color-bias per year. By 2002, the number had nearly tripled to 1,400 complaints of color-bias. This explosion may be related to increasing cases of discrimination, and it may also be evidence of increasing awareness that color-based discrimination is not only wrong, it's illegal.

Many cases of color-based discrimination have ended up in the courts. In 2002, the EEOC sued the owners of a Mexican restaurant in San Antonio, Texas for color-based discrimination. A white manager at the restaurant claimed that the owners directed him to hire only light-skinned staff to work in the dining room. The EEOC won the case and the restaurant was forced to pay $100,000 in fines.[6] In 2003, a dark-skinned African American won a claim of $40,000 from a national restaurant chain for color-based discrimination from a fellow black employee. The plaintiff argued that he suffered constant taunting and color-based epithets about his dark skin from lighter-skinned African American co-workers.[7] These are just two examples of how colorism affects people of color on a daily basis. Most people of color will not end up in court over color bias, but all people of color will experience or witness unfair treatment because of a person's skin tone.

Sociological research reveals that lighter-skinned African Americans and Mexican Americans earn more money, complete more years of education, live in more integrated neighborhoods, and have better mental health than do darker-skinned African Americans and Mexican Americans.[8] The long history of skin color stratification for both of these groups has its roots in their colonization and enslavement by Europeans. Europeans and white Americans created racial hierarchies to justify their subhuman treatment of the people of color they colonized and enslaved. This was the beginning of the ideology of white supremacy. The alleged superiority of whiteness, and all things approximating it including white or light skin, was the rule.

White racism is the fundamental building block of colorism, or skin color stratification, among Mexican Americans and African Americans. The maintenance of white supremacy in this country is predicated on the notion that dark skin represents savagery, irrationality, ugliness, and inferiority. White skin, and thus whiteness itself, is defined by the opposite: civility, rationality, beauty, and superiority.[9] These meanings are infused into actual body types to create the system of racism as we know it today.

> Racist ideology usually involves an esthetic appraisal of physical features, a mythology about traits of mind and personality correlated with physical features, and an almost mystical belief in the power of "blood" to elevate or to taint.[10]

Skin color and features associated with whites, such as light skin, straight noses, and long, straight hair, take on the meanings that they represent: civility, rationality, and beauty. Similarly, skin colors and features associated with Africans or Indians, such as dark skin, broad noses, and kinky hair, represent savagery, irrationality, and ugliness. The values associated with physical features set the stage for skin color stratification.

This study of color bias is further complicated by its simultaneous attention to sexism. I examine how skin color stratification specifically affects African American and Mexican American women in the areas of income, education, and the marriage market. This book allows the voices of real women to reveal how skin color has affected their lives as they describe the often, private hurt and pain on both sides of the color line. One woman I interviewed describes her frustration with men of color and their perceptions of beauty.

> In terms of models and catalogs, there are no black women, only white women.... I guess they're [black and Latino men] attracted to white women. I think they like more long hair, light eyes, lighter complexion. I know some Latino guys say, "I don't want no indigenous looking girl." Black guys are like, "I don't really like dark girls unless they have long hair." But not a lot of dark girls are going to have long hair. That's white girls. I think they like a lighter, closer to white variety of females.

Skin color bias creates many painful experiences for women of color, especially darker-skinned women. This has led many women to try to alter their appearances through skin bleaching creams, make-up application, use of colored contact lenses, dieting, hair straightening and hair extensions, and even cosmetic surgery. Many of these procedures have the effect of whitening or Anglicizing a woman's appearance in order to make her more "beautiful."[11]

In fact, the pursuit of light skin color can be so important it can prove fatal. A Harvard Medical School researcher found outbreaks of mercury poisoning in Saudi Arabia, Pakistan, Tanzania, and the southwestern United States. He came to learn that the poisoning, found almost exclusively in women, was caused by the widespread use of skin-bleaching creams containing toxic levels of mercury.[12] Children, too, suffered—either from in utero absorption during pregnancy, or from mothers who put the bleaching cream on their children eager for them to have the benefits of light skin, the more valued complexion.

Noted social scientist Vicki Ruiz describes the pressure from inside and outside of the Mexican American community for young women to pursue beauty and to wear cosmetics.

> The use of cosmetics, however, cannot be blamed entirely on Madison Avenue ad campaigns. The innumerable barrio beauty pageants, sponsored by mutualistas, patriotic societies, churches, the Mexican Chamber of Commerce, newspapers, and even progressive labor unions, encouraged young women to accentuate their physical attributes.[13]

Ruiz provides a persuasive example of the power of beauty to structure the lives of women. Her long list of Mexican organizations that support the ideology of beauty is alarming, especially because it includes organizations such as "churches" and "progressive labor unions." Her description of the pursuit of beauty, often in the name of ethnic pride (at ethnic festivals and celebrations), illustrates the inherent contradictions between racial pride and a pursuit of beauty than valorizes whiteness.

In her essay about young black women and their beauty attitudes and practices, sociologist Maxine Leeds describes the contradictory position many young black women find themselves in.

> These students frequently stated that there was a beauty standard that valued lighter skin and longer and straighter hair. They distanced themselves from that standard and articulated a more inclusive idea of beauty. Yet their own taunts about skin color and hair length indicate that they, to some degree, accept a Eurocentric ideal.[14]

She describes her interview participants as able to see beauty in traditionally black identities including dark skin color and short, natural hair, but it seems as if they have not completely released the power of the white ideal of beauty.[15] They stand outside of a white cultural ideal, yet they have internalized it. When Leeds asked the young women if there was anything they would change about their appearance, most responded with wanting longer hair, lighter skin or lighter eyes—all traits associated with whites and not blacks.

Another way in which sexism interacts with racism is in its structuring of the marriage market. Women learn to compete with one another for men in the marriage marketplace. Women compete with one another over many traits including educational credentials, income, family status, and perhaps most importantly, beauty. Skin color is closely tied to the definition of beauty such that light-skinned or white women are considered more "beautiful" than darker-skinned women of color.[16] In this way, beauty works as a form of social capital for women. Beauty is capital because it is transformable into other types of capital, such as economic capital or money.[17] The amount of beauty a woman possesses may help her land a well-paying job or marry a high-status, wealthy man.

But what about the Black is Beautiful movement and the Brown Pride movement? In the 1960s and 1970s many African Americans and Mexican Americans were involved in cultural revolutions that inverted the racist norms of white beauty and celebrated brown skin, African and Indian features, and natural hair. These movements were significant and were part and parcel of the larger struggles for political and economic rights. It was common to hear young Chicanos referring to "Aztec Goddesses" and young blacks to "Nubian Princesses." But this burgeoning aesthetic, though influential, did not create a substantial permanent change in American culture. Blacks and Chicanos will forever be imprinted with the proud messages of those days, but many of those values have become more talk than reality as skin-bleaching creams continue to be used and facial cosmetic surgery is on the rise among people of color.

How are lighter and darker women affected by their skin tone in the worlds of work, education, and the marriage market? Resources are allocated unequally to light and dark-skinned women and beauty  is constructed to elevate the status of light-skinned black and Mexican American women who most closely physically resemble whites. Skin color, racial, and gender hierarchies all work at the ideological level to construct beauty as a tool of patriarchy and racism. Because beauty is an ideology, its standards serve the interests of dominant social groups. In this case beauty is a hegemonic ideology and its existence serves the interests of whites in that it maintains white privilege. Beauty as an ideology also serves the interests of men because it maintains patriarchy as it divides women through competition and reduces their power.

The ideology of beauty is linked to ideologies of competence and intelligence. In a public sphere still debating racial differences in intelligence,[18] racial images that signify who "looks smart" are heavily influenced by race, gender, and skin color. People with light skin and Anglo features, usually associated with rationality and civility, are more likely to be perceived as intelligent and competent than are individuals with skin colors and features associated with Africans or Indians and thus associated with savagery, and incompetence.[19]

The status characteristics of race, color, and gender also work at the material level as they affect educational outcomes, income differences, and occupational characteristics of individuals and groups. Often through the ideological work discussed above, women are discriminated against both overtly and covertly in the worlds of work and education. For example, a light-skinned Mexican American woman is viewed by other Mexican Americans and by whites as higher status, less racially conscious (and therefore less threatening), more "respectable," and more assimilable than her darker-skinned counterparts. These perceptions give her a competitive edge in schools and job markets still tainted by racism.

On average, women, earn less money than men; people of color earn less than whites, and darker-skinned people of color earn less than lighter-skinned people of color. I will examine how these three social facts interact and make it so that darker-skinned Mexican American and African American women earn less, learn less, and marry those with less, than do their lighter, whiter counterparts.

## WHY STUDY SKIN COLOR?

Most sociological research on racism focuses on the position of various racial and ethnic groups relative to whites. Although that point is integral to this book, I will go further by showing how lighter-skinned people of color are privileged over darker-skinned people of color within racial/ethnic groups. In the case of skin color stratification within the black and Mexican American communities, white racism is the fundamental building block of that stratification, just as it is for stratification across the racial groups of white, black, Latino, Indian, Asian, and others.

The privilege of light-skinned African American and Mexican American women does not operate in the same way that race privilege operates for whites, but privilege operates nonetheless. I will describe the mechanisms of that system and their similarities and differences in both ethnic communities. When Spike Lee wrote and directed the film *School Daze,* which dealt with issues of skin color and black identity on a college campus, he was met with both praise and contempt. Many people thanked him for bringing to light the often hidden issue of colorism and sparking a larger public discussion of the topic. Others criticized him for "airing dirty laundry" and distracting the public from the more important issue of racial discrimination. I strongly believe that discussing skin color bias in the Mexican American and African American communities does not distract us from the important matter of racial discrimination. In fact, skin color stratification supports the contention that racial discrimination is alive and well, and so insidious that communities of color themselves are divided into quasi-racial hierarchies. Without a larger system of institutional racism, colorism based on skin tone would not exist. Colorism is part and parcel of racism and exists because of it.

How does a person with light skin end up with more education, a higher income, and a higher status spouse than a person with the same background characteristics, but with darker skin? This book attempts to answer that question by examining the history of racism and skin color bias, examining how skin tone affects women's income, educational attainment, and spouse's status, and uncovering how skin tone is tied to definitions of beauty and ethnic authenticity.

Systems of discrimination operate on at least two levels in terms of race and color. The first system of discrimination is the level of racial category (i.e., black, Asian, Indian, etc.). The second system of discrimination is at the level of skin tone—darker skin or lighter skin. These two systems of discrimination work in concert in white, black, and Chicano communities. Racism and colorism are responsible for discrimination against people because of their racial or ethnic identity, as well as for discrimination against dark-skinned people of color, and the privileging of light-skinned people of color. These two systems are distinct, but inextricably connected, because a light-skinned Mexican American woman may still experience racism, despite her light skin, and a dark-skinned Mexican American woman may experience racism and colorism simultaneously.

Where did these ideas about skin color come from? Historically, skin color affected the stereotypic racist, sexist, and sexual images produced during slavery and the colonization of the Americas. There are many familiar images such as the black Mammy (loyal servant), and the black Jezebel (whore), and their Mexican American counterparts—the deeply religious, pious, Mexican American mother, and the "hot tamale," promiscuous, Mexican or Mexican American woman. All of these images are informed by ideologies that define certain races, genders, and colors as subordinate.

These images are not just a thing of the past, however. Controlling images such as these influence our perceptions of beauty and our ability to acquire social capital. European domination of both Africans and Mexicans has left a legacy of seeing beauty only in whiteness, and of using beauty as a method of objectifying women's bodies. If beauty is for women, what "brains" are for men, then how do women use their beauty as social capital and convert it into other forms of capital such as economic resources? I will show that the emphasis on women's bodies as commodities, coupled with a tendency to attribute other positive characteristics to people who possess beauty creates a market-like system where women can invest in their own beauty, as human capital, to increase their employability, their marriage ability, and their quality of life. It is also important to investigate how racism works to unequally allocate resources to women with various skin tones. In chapter 3, I will discuss how personal incomes, educational attainment, and even the status of one's spouse are determined in part by a woman's skin tone.

As is true with most feminist research, the goal of this book is to produce knowledge for social change. Resisting racism and sexism is an ongoing battle and I hope that this book provides knowledge and purpose toward that end. The goal of many feminist researchers is to transform the existing social world.

> Underlying much of the reflexivity found in feminist scholarship is the notion found in the earlier work of scholars such as W. E. B. Du Bois (1969) and Paulo Friere (1970) that consciousness of oppression can lead to a creative insight that is generated by experiencing contradictions (often at life's "rupture points"). Under ideal circumstances transformation occurs, during which something hidden is revealed about the formerly taken-for-granted aspects of sexual asymmetry. Thus, in this model, previously-hidden phenomena which are apprehended as a contradiction can lead to one or more of the following: an emotional catharsis...; an academic insight and resulting intellectual product; and increased politicization and corresponding activism.[20]

The research process itself can be a consciousness-raising experience for all involved. Ideally, the researchers, writers, participants, interviewees, and readers all gain an opportunity, through the research project, to reflect on social injustice. This reflection may lead to further understanding of one's own situation and/or a heightened sense of politicization. The most important purpose of this book is to produce alternative intellectual ways of understanding racism and sexism, and to compel people to act against these systems in their own creative ways.

## WHERE FEMINIST THEORY MEETS RACE THEORY

The challenge of conducting a study that encompasses the works of several different disciplines (i.e., sociology, history, psychology, women's studies, Chicano and Chicana studies, and African American studies) is formulating a theory to encompass the wide variety of perspectives and experiences in this project. As postmodern theory has taught us, there is no one grand narrative that can explain all of social life for all people. Therefore, I have used strands from several different theoretical frameworks, all woven together to provide the most comprehensive and eclectic understanding of this project.

First, the entire racial analysis in this project is situated in historical perspective. In chapter 2, I outline the history of colonization for Mexican Americans beginning with the Spanish conquistadoras and including the present U.S. imperialism in Mexico and in the Mexican American community here in the United States. I also outline the history of the domination of African Americans beginning with slavery in the United States and including present day exploitation and discrimination. Situating each analysis in a historical perspective allows us to theorize about how slavery and colonialism created systems of racism that are still alive today.

Also included in this theoretical framework is the concept of the "racial project" from Michael Omi and Howard Winant.[21] I use their notion of the racial project to describe the changing nature of race relations in the United States and the continual presence of skin color stratification within ethnic communities. Based on the struggle for power in society, racial categories are manipulated and transformed to guarantee one segment of the population, whites, the largest portion of resources. Consequently, the boundaries of the races are always changing and who is included in which category changes with politics, economics, and the historical moment.

In both the African American and Mexican American communities, struggles over the definitions of whiteness and "otherness" have raged.[22] For instance, the Rule of Hypodescent,[23] stating that anyone with "one drop of black blood" is legally black, may be seen as a racial project that broadly defined the identity of blacks in order to create more enslavable people. Later, after slavery was abolished, the Rule of Hypodescent was maintained by whites to decrease the competition for scarce resources and shut blacks out of the political process.

The racial boundaries defining Mexican Americans have also been transformed over time. Mexican Americans were often considered to be Indians and thus excluded from formal participation in politics and the economy. However, when it was in the interest of Anglos in the Southwest to do business with Mexican people and to have access to their wealth, they defined them as white.[24] The changing racial definitions for Mexican Americans and African Americans are examples of the "racial projects" concept that I employ in this study.

This book also engages feminist standpoint theory as articulated by scholars such as Dorothy Smith, Sandra Harding, and Patricia Hill Collins.[25] I use standpoint theory as a way to ground my analysis and "study up." I begin from the lives of Mexican American and African American women and generate sociological problems and questions from that standpoint. "But though women's experiences can generate important problems, they do not offer any answers; the determinants of women's daily experience are not to be found in that experience, but elsewhere—in the political, economic, and social order."[26] I apply Smith's ideas by using women of color's experiences with beauty and social capital as a starting point for my analysis. I then look for explanations for these experiences in the larger systems of sexism, racism, and capitalism.

In addition, the theory of intersectionality completes my theoretical framework of understanding race, color, and gender in the lives of African American and Mexican American women.[27] The concept of intersectionality is key to this project because it allows the researcher to weave various grand theories, such as feminism and postcolonial theory, together to create new and specific theories of oppression. For instance, cultural critic bell hooks (1981) does this in her explanation of black women's unique oppression under slavery.[28] She writes that black women were dominated by patriarchy, experiencing a second-class status to black men and to white women. Yet, black women did not receive the "protections" of patriarchy—freedom from hard work, sexual protection, etc.—because they were black. Sexism is experienced differently for women of different racial and ethnic backgrounds.

Because this study focuses on women of color it is imperative to understand how race and gender interact in their lives and create specific kinds of racial and gendered oppression.[29] Deborah King points out that oppression is not simply additive as in "race + gender," but instead it is muliplicative in the sense that race and gender multiply and create new systems of oppression, and different manifestations of oppression that do not exist for others.[30] One of the ways in which I discuss intersectionality is in the sexualization of racism. Sexism and racism interact to create an additional form of oppression that is focused on sexuality. Through this black women and Mexican American women are depicted as sexually insatiable, debased, and dirty. The practice of raping women of color (a significant problem throughout American history) serves patriarchal interests in oppressing women and serves racial interests as well by terrorizing entire communities of color. This is just one example of how race and gender oppressions can interact to create new monsters.

## WHY COMPARE AFRICAN AMERICANS
## AND MEXICAN AMERICANS?

Of all the diverse communities in the United States, why focus on African Americans and Mexican Americans when studying colorism? Although they have many differences, Mexican Americans and African Americans have an important similarity in that they are the two largest racial/ethnic minority groups in the United States. For this reason alone it is important to ascertain what they have in common and how their experiences with racism and sexism are similar and different.

Both Mexican Americans and African Americans have a history of white domination and both groups are racially marked as non-white. Both groups also have a wide variety of skin tones resulting from a history of mixture and intermarriage with other populations—primarily whites and Indians for African Americans, and primarily Spanish (Europeans), indigenous people, and Africans for the Mexican American population.

To begin my comparative analysis, I outline the relevant historical events for both African American and Mexican American women and place them in a theoretical framework that explains race as an ever-changing social category, and a category that is different for various racial groups. I also outline the process of racialization and the ideological, social, economic, political, historical, and cultural work that must be done to maintain it. Next, I articulate the intersections of race, gender, and color through an ideological lens and examine how sexual images of both groups of women have been used against them. I also examine the construction of beauty and the commodification of women in the marriage market. By using this comparative framework to study race, color, and gender, I am able to expose the continuities of racism across groups and circumstances, as well as the different ways that racism manifests itself in each of these ethnic communities.

Although there are many good reasons to compare these two groups, there is one significant sticking point: Are Mexican Americans a race? Sociologists typically define racial groups as differing in physical characteristics, while ethnic groups are defined by their cultural practices.[31] I believe arguments may be made for viewing African Americans and Mexican Americans as both racial and ethnic groups. Conventional wisdom defines black people as only physically different from whites, but there are also many cultural practices from Africa, the Caribbean, and other regions, as well as those developed here in the United States, that make African Americans culturally distinct from other groups.

Similarly, many Mexican Americans possess physical characteristics that differentiate them from Anglos, but they also have many cultural practices that are unique to their own Mexican and Indian heritage, as well as those that they share with other Latino peoples. Therefore, I will use both terms—racial groups and ethnic groups—to refer to African Americans and Mexican Americans throughout this study.

## THE NUTS AND BOLTS: DATA AND METHODS

I take a multi-method approach to studying the intersections of race, color, and gender in the lives of African American and Mexican American women. I have used both quantitative analysis of survey data and qualitative interviewing techniques to gain the broadest understanding possible of the issues around color, race, and gender for black and Chicana women.

The quantitative data analysis utilizes two national data sets, the National Survey of Black Americans (NSBA), and the National Chicano Survey (NCS).[32] Both of these data sets are national random samples structured to accurately represent the diversity of African American and Mexican American people in the United States. Between the two data sets nearly two thousand women are included in this portion of the study. I use multivariate regression analyses to investigate how skin color affects three outcome variables: earnings, educational attainment, and spousal status. Through this analysis I will show that lighter-skinned African American women are rewarded with more resources and more status than are darker-skinned women. I will also show that lighter-skinned Mexican American women are rewarded with more resources and more status than are darker-skinned women, but in a slightly different way than black women.

The qualitative data analysis uses data from open-ended, one-on-one interviews that I conducted with twenty-six Mexican American and African American female college students. From these twenty-six interviews I gathered information on how each group of women defines beauty, defines ethnic group membership, and feels about the role of color in the dating and marriage markets.

As is true in any face-to-face interaction, racial identity played a role. I am a light-skinned, biracial, African American woman who could pass for white. This presented both benefits and challenges in the process. I spoke candidly before each interview about my own color and my interest in the color politics in the Mexican American and African American communities. I assured the women I spoke with that they could speak candidly about their feelings without fear of "hurting my feelings" or "making me uncomfortable." "I've heard it all before," I told them. Nonetheless, I am sure that if I had a darker complexion, I would have had a different type of access to some women's feelings. My Spanish language skills are also fairly rudimentary which slightly limited the fluid communication with Chicana participants. Although all of the Chicanas I interviewed were fluent English speakers, several often used Spanish sayings about skin color to help convey their points. They always translated them, but something is usually lost in translation. Despite these limitations, I feel very confident that the women I interviewed spoke honestly and freely and enjoyed the interview process. I think the excerpts speak for themselves in showing the high-level of rapport that was established between myself and the interviewees.

The interviews show that even in very different communities, the participants' definitions of beauty were very similar, consistently valuing lightness and whiteness. Also, women in both groups felt that lighter skin was also a sign of weak group membership and generated low levels of race consciousness for blacks and Mexican Americans. Lastly, the politics of color were a significant issue in family life for the Mexican American participants. Among the African American participants, color was a cause of problems in female friendships. These and other issues will be discussed in chapters 5 and 6.

## LAYOUT OF THE BOOK

Chapter 2 focuses on the history of colonization and patriarchy for African Americans and Mexican Americans. During slavery, jobs on the plantation were often assigned by skin color, creating animosity among the slaves. This was a "divide and conquer" strategy used to prevent revolts. Many elite African American organizations later internalized and perpetuated these ideologies by adopting color rules that excluded darker-skinned people from participation. Similarly, in "New Spain" skin colors were rank ordered and lightness was highly valued. Despite high levels of racial mixture and intermarriage (unlike in the United States) the ideology of mestizaje developed alongside, and did not displace, a stringent racial/color hierarchy. Examining definitions of beauty in this context show how light skin is deeply implicated in an "aesthetic of whiteness."

Chapter 3 is the quantitative analysis of survey data. This chapter surveys much of the quantitative data analysis done on skin color in the Mexican American and African American communities to date. Multivariate regression analysis of survey data reveals that lighter-skinned African American and Mexican American women complete more years of education, earn higher personal incomes, and marry higher status spouses than do darker-skinned women with similar background characteristics. The data for this chapter are taken from two national survey data sets: the National Survey of Black Americans and the National Chicano Survey.

Chapter 4 is an investigation of racism and cosmetic surgery. Just as skin color matters in status acquisition, so do facial features. For many years, skin color and facial features were permanent traits that could not be easily or significantly changed. However, with the growing popularity of cosmetic surgery, the past ten years have seen a surge in procedures that alter women's bodies in myriad ways. Cosmetic surgeries that alter "ethnic" features such as thick lips, broad noses, or eye shape and make those features more European or Anglo are steadily growing in popularity. This chapter investigates this new trend and its implications for racial stratification.

 Chapter 5 is based on data from the twenty-six qualitative interviews with African American and Mexican American women. Women from both groups, of all colors, discussed the advantages of light skin: high status in the ethnic community, being defined as beautiful, and desirability in the dating/marriage market. There were also some significant differences in African American and Mexican American women's experiences. African American women experienced high levels of tension and jealousy over skin color in female friendships. Mexican American women, on the other hand, experienced feelings of pain and betrayal when family members evaluated their beauty and color in relation to other family members

Chapter 6, an examination of ethnic authenticity, further analyzes the data from the qualitative interviews. The most significant disadvantage of light skin, reported by light-skinned women across the board, was the perception that they were not "ethnic enough." Light and dark women from both groups reported that light skin was not consistent with an image of being "truly" African American or Mexican American and many reported being rejected by co-ethnic peers for not being black or Chicano "enough." Spanish language use was also closely connected to ethnic authenticity for Mexican American participants causing extreme stress for those whose Spanish language skills were weak or absent altogether.

Chapter 7 is the concluding chapter and describes the resistance to and entrenchment of colorism. Despite the fact that light skin is widely valued in the African American and Mexican American communities, many women of color are also challenging the normative value of light skin. Second, changing racial dynamics, spurred in part by the influx of new immigrants to the United States, are affecting the process of color-ism. In the future, color may not be an "immutable" characteristic. Social class may begin to affect perceptions of color, much the way it does in Latin America. Or, in the future, color may be "compensated for" with other high-status characteristics. Lastly, I suggest that future research might include women of other ethnic and racial groups to determine in what ways they experience colorism, if at all.

# 2

## THE COLOR OF SLAVERY AND CONQUEST

How do we begin to unravel the tightly woven matrix of race, color, and history that seems to predate almost everything we know? Is there a point of origin for colorism that we can find? I argue that the European colonial project in the Americas and the trafficking of Africans as slaves set the stage, both ideologically and materially, for the systems of racism and colorism we now know. Because Europeans and European Americans used their power to culturally, politically, and economically dominate Africans and Mexicans (including indigenous people of the Americas), they created a "white is right" culture that served to support their colonial and slave society endeavors. In this chapter, I try to unravel how each of these systems got started and how racism spawned colorism—the system of assigning value to people by the lightness or darkness of their skin color within racial groups.

### AFRICAN AMERICANS

One of the key phenomena to understanding skin color stratification among African Americans is the history of sexual violence against African women by white men during slavery. "The social order established by powerful white men was founded on two inseparable ingredients: the dehumanization of Africans on the basis of race, and the control of women's sexuality and reproduction."[1] As one of the violent mechanisms of social control that whites exercised against African Americans, sexual violence, including rape, was part of the beginning of the skin color stratification process itself. This violent method of social control produced two important effects. The first and most obvious result was the creation of racially mixed children by white fathers and black mothers. The second more long-term effect was the creation of a color hierarchy through systematic privileging of light-skinned African Americans over darker-skinned African Americans. Though many mixed-race offspring were the result of violent unions between white men and black women, there were also a notable number of consensual relationships between the races. Many men and women involved in interracial relationships lived together and were married in churches despite an enormous amount of resistance on the part of most whites and some blacks.[2]

The first effect of white sexual violence, increasing the diversity of skin tones among the black population, is very closely tied to the Rule of Hypodescent. During the enslavement of African Americans, the Rule of Hypodescent, or the One Drop Rule, was used to determine who was black and who was not. The One Drop Rule defined all people with "one drop of black blood" as members of the black race.[3] This policy was first developed to ensure that there would be a surplus of people who, by being defined as black, could be "legally" enslaved. Later, the rule was used to limit black access to resources, to limit black political power, and to maintain the myth of white racial purity. Because virtually all mixed-race people were identified as black, they were unable to vote (effectively until 1965), prevented from working in many occupations, and excluded from attending most universities.[4] This meant that there was less competition for whites over a finite amount of resources. Additionally, the myth of white racial purity was a strong ideological tenet of the early United States that required constant vigilance and boundary maintenance. Interracial relationships were illegal and individuals suspected of engaging in them were often punished harshly. Many African Americans, especially men, were lynched because of rumor or reality of relations with a white woman.

The Rule of Hypodescent is inextricably linked to the gender politics that surround race. One of the primary motivations for the One Drop Rule was to maintain "race purity," and the keepers of the white race were white women. White men controlled white women's sexuality and reproduction in order to maintain their patriarchal power over them and to maintain a sense of race purity by monitoring with whom white women had sexual relations. This form of "protecting" white womanhood became the centerpiece of a campaign of lynching black men—all done to justify keeping the white race pure.

Similarly, black women were the centerpiece for blackness—any child born to a black mother was defined as black. During slavery it enabled white men to rape black women in order to produce more slaves.[5]

Although rape was used as a method to create more "enslaveable" people, it was used more commonly as a tool of terrorism to control the actions and rebellions of both black men and women. The race of a child was always defined by the mother because paternity was never certain, but maternity was. The combined effect of the One Drop Rule and the systematic rape of African American women by white men created a larger population of African Americans with various skin tones,[6] and most notably, a significant number of very light-skinned black people.

The second primary effect of sexual violence during slavery was to systematically privilege lighter-skinned blacks via their connection with the white slave owner and thus their connection with whiteness. Overseers and members of the slave owning family often gave racially mixed children special status because they were the offspring of a white slave owner. Opportunities for manumission, less violent treatment by overseers, less stressful work tasks, access to education, and opportunities for skilled labor are all examples of the privileges that lighter-skinned black children often received.[7]

With the option of privileges, such as occasional manumission, a growing class of free light-skinned blacks began to emerge even before the end of slavery in the United States.[8] Many of these people were ex-slaves freed by their white slave owners/fathers, while others were free blacks who had never been slaves. "In 1850, mulattos or mixed bloods constituted 37% of the free Negro population."[9] This population of Freedmen was able to gain skills and to become modest business people in many major Southern cities. This was the beginning of an African American light-skinned elite in the contemporary United States.[10]

In the post-Civil War era, the growing class of light-skinned Freedmen found itself poised to lead the now free African American population. Many Freedmen served as leaders of local business, church, and civic, organizations.[11] They were able to take up positions of leadership more easily than many other African Americans because they had been free and often economically established for years.[12] Many whites interpreted the emergence of this light-skinned African American leadership as confirmation that white blood and lineage was superior to black. Many whites saw the notable success of mixed-race and light-skinned people as evidence that only those with "white blood" had the capacity to lead. They understood there to be a direct relationship between the proportion of white ancestry one had and his or her intellectual capabilities.

E. B. Reuter's (in)famous work *The Mulatto in the United States* is an example of that type of racist thinking.[13] He asserts that mixed-race African Americans have emerged as leaders of the black community because of their genetic likeness to whites instead of the opportunity structure available to them as light-skinned descendants of Freedmen. This kind of genetic thinking explains why light skin is associated with superior abilities, particularly intellectual ones. It harkens all the way back to scientific racism that endorsed the ideas of genetic racial proportions correlating with intelligence.[14]

## AFRICAN RACIALIZATION

The legacies of European colonialism and African American enslavement are manifest in the racialization of African Diaspora communities in the United States.[15] One of the most important characteristics of a slave system is its racial nature. "Slavery was racial. By the 1700s, slavery was a racial status suitable only for Africans and persons of African descent."[16] The racialization of Africans was the result of a racist ideology employed by many European nations to justify the enslavement and inhuman treatment of African people. This European ideological position was the beginning of the colonial mentality adopted by whites in the United States.

The process of racialization for African Americans can be understood through racial formation theory.[17] Racial formation theory describes a process through which racial categories are constructed and altered over time. Racial projects establish what "race" means in any given historical period through images, representations, and explanations about racial categories or groups. These racial meanings are then used to justify organizing a society along racial lines and to disperse resources accordingly. This theory works well to explain how racist ideologies came to represent African Americans in negative ways and then went on to allocate resources according to the racial meanings of the day.

Racist ideologies were central to the justification of slavery in the United States. These ideologies defined the races in opposition to one another: Black people and blackness were defined as barbaric, savage, heathen and ugly; white people and whiteness were defined as civilized, modern, Christian, and beautiful.[18] This kind of ideology and its symbolism were necessary for the Europeans to justify their treatment of the Africans they brought over from Africa. All public discourse on issues of race or slavery was then engaged through this lens of racial binarisms and oppositions, with blackness always being defined negatively.

Through this racist ideology, "African-ness" came to be known as evil and "whiteness" came to be known as virtuous. These abstract concepts, however, quickly manifest themselves in the actual phenotypic characteristics of the racial groups. For instance, Drake's use of the term "Negroidness" refers to a construct of African physicality that has inspired "esthetic derogation" by white racism.[19] Blackness and whiteness were no longer merely abstract concepts. Actual physical traits associated with each racial group began to take on these ideological meanings. Dark brown skin, kinky hair, and broad noses started to represent barbarism and ugliness. Similarly, straight blonde hair and white skin began to represent civility and beauty.

This shift of meaning from the abstract concepts of whiteness and blackness to the actual physical traits of the races is at the crux of the contemporary phenomenon of skin color stratification. Phenotypic characteristics are now the representations of the racist ideologies of the early American and European colonialists. Seeing some facial features as representing barbarism and ugliness and other features as representing modernity and beauty, and the consequential valuation of lightness over darkness, is an important mechanism through which contemporary skin color stratification occurs and is perpetuated in the United States.

## MEXICAN AMERICANS

For Mexican Americans, the historical context of skin color differentiation and stratification begins with the Spanish colonization of Mexico. As a part of Europe, Spain was involved in the creation of colonial, racist ideology and propaganda to justify its movement into Africa, Latin America, and other parts of the non-white world. "New Spain" was a hierarchical multi-ethnic society that included Spanish Europeans, indigenous peoples, and Africans who were enslaved by the Europeans. This multi-ethnic society was the setting for the process of racialization that the Spanish instigated in order to justify their conquest and colonization of Mesoamerica.[20] As discussed earlier, the racialization of Africans in the United States occurred throughout their enslavement. The process of racializing the "Indians," the indigenous peoples of New Spain, was a different task altogether that would require the commingling of the racist ideologies of the Spanish, as well as the white American ideology of Manifest Destiny.[21]

The Spanish constructed a racial hierarchy where white Europeans dominated all other peoples of color. Through typical modes of colonization, the Spanish stole land, demolished governments, and continuously suppressed the indigenous peoples. As was true for most European colonizers, the Spanish justified their pillaging of the land and people with an ideology portraying themselves as civilized Christians on a mission to save the savage and heathen dark "Other." Similarities to the previous discussion of the racialization of Africans in the United States are obvious. Whites labeled both Mexican Americans and African Americans as heathens, barbaric, and generally as Other. The way that the groups were negatively characterized coupled with their physical differences constituted the racialization of these groups by whites. Whites saw the negative traits they associated with Africans and Mexicans as natural and genetic, thus making whites naturally superior (in their own minds) to the Mexican and African people.

However, one of the major differences in how the two societies developed was the level of intermarriage and mixture of the ethnic/racial groups.[22] Some of these relationships were consensual, but many were through violence. There were many "reports of atrocities committed against the native populations, especially against the Indian women."[23] Rape was a common form of Spanish social control in New Spain, and indigenous women were the most common victims. "The sexual and other violence toward Amerindian women in California can best be understood as ideologically justified violence institutionalized in the structures and relations of conquest."[24] The rape and sexual terrorization of women of color by white colonizers is central to the race-gender relations that have evolved today. The view of women as property that could be desecrated in military conflicts set the stage for seeing women of color today as objects and not subjects.

The combination of white Spanish men raping Indian women and the number of consensual relationships resulted in a racially mixed population like no other, and the *mestizo* was born. The process of racial mixing, or whitening, was an overt socio-political project with the goal of raising the status of Mexico in the eyes of Europe, despite its significant indigenous and African populations. This process of creating *mestizaje* was so popular, in fact, that it was the subject of scores of paintings in the eighteenth and nineteenth centuries called *castas*. Artists' paintings typically included a man, woman, and child with racial descriptions of each. The viewer assumes the threesome is a family and the paintings show the results of various racial combinations. For instance, an anonymous painter created a picture titled "Mulatto and Spaniard, Produce Morisco" or "Mulatto and Mestiza Produce a Mulatto Return-Backwards."[25] Titles like the latter, by Juan Rodriguez Juarez, suggest that sometimes the offspring of a mixed union will "return backwards" and look more like the darker parent. The discourse of this genre belies the thinking of the time that racial whitening was a positive step "forward" for Mexicans while dark skin was still associated with barbarism and inferiority. Today, Mexico considers itself a mestizo population with no "races" per se, yet there still remains a debilitating color-caste system left over from the colonial days of New Spain. This color-caste system has been adopted and reinforced through Mexican elites and contemporary U.S. influence.

Eventually, the Spanish were overthrown, and in 1821 Mexico won the revolution and re-established itself as an independent nation. As Mexico began to re-create its own national identity it struggled with the developing discourse of scientific racism. Scientific racism was a European theory stating that races of people were scientific realities and that the darker the race of people the more ignorant and incapable they were. Whiteness was re-affirmed as a superior race, but this time with the backing of hegemonic European scientific racism.

This posed a serious problem for many Latin American countries that had a mixture of races and cultures resulting from colonization and trade. This was the case for Mexico. They wanted to be considered a country of leadership and intelligence, but they also had many brown skinned peoples—mestizos. World renowned Mexican philosopher Jose Vasconcelos developed the theory of *la raza cosmica*—the cosmic race.[26] He argued that mestizos constituted a race of their own, not just a mixture of others. "The social genius of *La Raza* as Vasconcelos envisioned it was in the model (the attitude) that it embraces the four major races of the world... *La Raza's* contribution was its concept of mestizaje. It was an inclusivistic model of social-racial integration."[27] Because the mestizo is a hybrid, Vasconcelos believed mestizos would be a superior race that would develop to exceed the limits of all other races including the white Europeans.

Vasconcelos was reacting to the scientific racism of the time that purported whites were the superior race. He was extremely critical of North American racism and imperialism. His work was an obvious threat to the racial order in the United States and Europe evidenced by the fact that it was not translated into English until over fifty years after it was written. Although Vasconcelos stood in opposition to scientific racism, his theory remained within the framework and discourse of eugenics. Nonetheless, his theory and the pride it instilled in the Mexican people came to be known as *La Raza*. This term is still used today. It no longer necessarily holds the meanings of racial superiority that it once did, but it remains a symbol of pride in a world, particularly for Mexican Americans, where a discourse of white superiority persists.

Meanwhile, the United States, true to its Puritan ideology of Manifest Destiny was waiting for the right opportunity to increase its land mass and take over part of Mexico. "European Americans saw it as their providential mission to settle the entire North American continent with a homogenous white population, bringing with them their superior political institutions, notions of progress and democracy, and economic system."[28] The idea of Manifest Destiny as articulated through white racism rests on the assumption of white superiority over all other peoples of color, including Mexicans. Manifest Destiny commingled strains of racism and capitalism to create an ideology that justified a massive land grab and oppression of American Indians and Mexicans.

Spurred by Manifest Destiny, a series of wars, trades, and deals ensued between the United States and Mexico, the most ideologically important of which was the Mexican-American War. One of the U.S. government's strategies to win the war was to flood the Southwest with Anglos. This created a situation where Mexicans in that area increasingly were seen as ethnic minorities in their own previous homeland. After the war, the border shifted southward and Mexicans were "renamed" Mexican Americans.

## *The American Re-Racialization of Mexicans*

Although Anglos recognized Mexican people as racially different from themselves, they saw enough similarity with them to consider maintaining economic and social relationships. "The Mexicans' mixed European ancestry, romance language, Catholic religious practices, and familiar political-economic institutions elevated them above all other cultural groups in the white man's eyes."[29] In fact, a significant debate developed over the racial status and thus citizenship rights of Mexicans in California after the signing of the Treaty of Guadalupe Hildalgo. The treaty stated that all Mexicans who chose to stay in the United States after the Mexican-American War would be granted full rights of citizenship. However, the ambiguous racial status of the Mexicans served as a future justification for denying Mexicans those rights.

The Mexican population in the United States reflected the color hierarchies of both countries. There were light-skinned *rancheros* who owned land, as well as darker-skinned laborers who looked more indigenous in skin color and facial features. This color and class distinction complicated the debate over the race and citizenship of Mexicans. Anglos were more willing to grant citizenship to wealthy, land-owning, light-skinned Mexican people than they were to poor or working class, dark-skinned Mexicans. And, color and class were still significantly correlated. The combination of color and class proved a serious disadvantage for working-class Mexican men and women because the U.S. courts, run almost entirely by whites, had no common race or class status with them and consequently no interest in helping them attain citizen status.[30]

The debate over the racial status of Mexican Americans has continued throughout the twentieth century. The various legal cases dealing with the racial identity of Mexican Americans have been extremely inconsistent.

Anglo judges would declare Mexicans as whites when it disabled them from demanding minority rights and later would declare them non-white when it restricted their access to rights reserved for whites only.[31] Mexican Americans were then stuck in a racial no-man's-land where they were unable to rally for minority rights as African Americans were, and simultaneously were unable to enjoy the privileges of whiteness as Anglos were.

The debate about the racial status of Mexican Americans persists even today, particularly in the context of immigration and assimilation. Scholars have been carefully observing the assimilation patterns of Mexican immigrants, and a significant debate has developed around whether this group of immigrants will assimilate into Anglo society as European immigrants did in the past, or if they will remain marginalized from dominant Anglo society like African Americans.[32] This debate is significant because the outcome will affect how Mexicans are racially categorized. Will they assimilate into Anglo society like earlier European immigrants and become racially white or will they continue to be discriminated against and become black? This debate is problematic because in either case the Mexican immigration experience is being interpreted through the over-simplified black/white racial paradigm. In sum, although it is not overt, the coded messages of the debate over Mexican assimilation reveal an unfulfilled need to racially categorize Mexicans once and for all.

### Being (Non)American and Raced

The first half of the twentieth century was a time of increased urbanization and industrialization in the United States and served as a backdrop for the way in which Mexican Americans continued to be racialized. Through a lens of "American-ness," and "whiteness" Mexican Americans were purposefully created as outsiders to that identity, as non-Americans. A racial project was launched to create an image of Mexicans and Mexican Americans as outsiders to the United States and as an economic threat to U.S. working people. Immigration and issues of the United States-Mexico border began to define the debate about Mexican Americans and their status as a racial minority group or as an assimilating ethnic group.

Immigration between the United States and New Spain, and later Mexico, has been a constant feature of history for both countries. Although Mexican people have been moving to and from the United States ever since their land was stolen, Mexicans also lived in the United States before many European whites. The migration of Mexican people was always mediated by U.S. labor needs. This manifested itself in events such as the Bracero Program (1942–1964), a temporary labor program created to use Mexican workers, almost exclusively men, to fill wartime labor shortages in the United States. Because of the constant flow of immigration from Mexico and the systemic xenophobia of the U.S. populace, Mexican-origin people were usually defined and described as Others—foreigners, non-Americans.

The identity of Mexican Americans, as defined by whites, was that of the non-American. This ideology was so strong among Anglos that the U.S. government was able to enact several mass relocations of Mexican Americans and Mexicans to Mexico. One of the reasons for the "repatriation" was the Great Depression. In an economic crisis, racial minorities are often scapegoated and blamed for hard times. In this case, Mexicans and Mexican Americans were not only blamed, but were also forcibly removed from the country. The fact that this repatriation took place with little resistance from the rest of the American public reinforces the idea that Mexican Americans were never seen as full U.S. citizens and that their identities as racialized people hinged on their identity as non-Americans. Amazingly, this same kind of repatriation is happening again in California in 2004. The Immigration and Naturalization Service has begun locating undocumented immigrants and forcibly deporting them.[33] The more things change, the more they stay the same.

## THE STANDPOINT OF WOMEN OF COLOR

I use feminist standpoint theory to study the intersections of race, gender, and color. This theory and method are necessary to shift the focus away from sociological topics that are male-centered, in order to reveal and then study topics that are central to women, such as the politics of beauty. "Women's daily experience must generate the 'problems' requiring sociological explanation. It provides the starting point for a more adequate sociology."[34] By positioning the analysis from the lives of women of color, specifically Mexican American and African American women, sociological problems come to the fore, such as the racial nature of the beauty industry. Instead of seeing an innocent variety of methods for coloring one's eyes and hair, we see a variety of methods to emulate the aesthetic of white women. These manipulations alter physical appearances to more closely approximate whiteness. This process is only visible from a woman of color's standpoint in the social world.

"One fundamental feature of this struggle for a self-defined standpoint involves tapping sources of everyday, unarticulated consciousness that have traditionally been denigrated in white, male controlled institutions."[35] Collins describes what is central to standpoint theory and what makes it revolutionary for women of color: It can see social problems that are invisible to mainstream sociology. The issues of beauty and internalized racism are perfect examples of "everyday, unarticulated consciousnesses" that have previously gone unexamined.

Beauty is typically defined in the United States, and increasingly around the world, by whiteness and Western-European features. "There is a surprisingly high level of agreement about who is beautiful and who is not."[36] Although the overt racial standards of beauty are often unspoken, people across ethnic groups and class levels tend to agree about who possesses beauty and who does not. Because beauty is a racist construct many women of color are not viewed as beautiful by mainstream society and thus do not possess beauty as a form of capital.

Beauty is a crucial resource for women. In fact, beauty operates at the level of social capital[37] for women in that it is transformable into other types of capital, such as economic capital or money. Naomi Wolf, author of the best-selling book *The Beauty Myth*, argues that by the 1980s, when professional women had made significant inroads into corporations and management positions, beauty became as important as intellectual qualifications for employment.[38] "Beauty was no longer just a symbolic form of currency; it literally *became* money."[39] Although Wolf argues vehemently about the ideology of beauty as oppressive for women, she never tackles the racial nature of the beauty industry. Wolf is not able to see, or avoids discussing, how current definitions of beauty serve not only a sexist agenda, but also a powerful and exclusive racial agenda.

Beauty as capital operates similarly to law professor Cheryl Harris's conception of "whiteness as property."[40] In discussing the phenomenon of racially "passing" she describes the, "valorization of whiteness as treasured property in a society structured on racial caste…the set of assumptions, privileges, and benefits that accompany the status of being white have become a valuable asset—one that whites sought to protect and those who passed sought to attain, by fraud if necessary."[41] Harris succinctly illustrates the importance of seeing whiteness as property, as a form of capital, by using terms such as "value" and "asset" when describing it. Whiteness, which is part and parcel of beauty, is a form of capital just as beauty is a form of capital.

St. Clair Drake and Horace R. Cayton interviewed black residents of Chicago in 1945 and asked them about the importance of skin color for women. Although the attitudes are from an older generation, few things have changed today. "I prefer a light person for a sweetheart or a wife.… They are usually more attractive; they're prettier; they have good hair. They're more intelligent."[42] This interview was done over fifty years ago, before the modern Civil Rights Movement, and amazingly, attitudes about women's beauty remain relatively unchanged. The fact that a woman possesses beauty, defined by light skin and "good" (meaning straight) hair is then used to extrapolate that she is also intelligent. This is an example of beauty as social capital, as it is transformable into perceived human capital (intelligence) that may yield more money through employment, education, or marriage.

Beauty also maintains patriarchy at its most basic level because its essence is female presentation for the male gaze. This is especially true in the marriage market. The construction of beauty around phenotypically white traits is central to the way beauty manifests itself in the marriage market. This kind of aesthetic "commodifies women by measuring various quantities of beauty that women broker in the marital marketplace."[43] Beauty is one of the most important criteria for competition in the marital marketplace.[44] The "traditional status advantage of light-skinned [African American] women holds for all cohorts, with little indication of change."[45] For black men, however, there has been significant change in the importance of light skin color. Their ability to attract light-skinned, high-status wives, and to be upwardly mobile is no longer as dependent on light skin color as it once was, and currently is for black women.[46]

Skin tone hierarchies among women have resulted in what I call "the beauty queue." In the beauty queue, the most beautiful women, which by definition must be the whitest and lightest, are placed at the front of the queue. Consequently, the darkest women, the women of color, are at the back of the queue, defined as "not beautiful." This queue is a kind of rank ordering of women for jobs or marriage partners. I will discuss this concept in more detail in chapter 5.

In an interview with researchers Robin Lakoff and Racquel Scherr, a Mexican woman reported feeling "ugly" because of her dark skin. "'I was called 'indita' or 'negrita'...I was ugly, no doubt about that...So ugly and so dark that I wasn't to go out in the sun'."[47] The racist nature of the construction of beauty is particularly apparent here. The interviewee reports being disparagingly called a "negrita" or an "indita" which literally means, "little black one" or "little Indian one." This is not simply a way of saying someone is ugly, or dark-skinned, but these labels racialize and stigmatize the person they are directed toward. They are thinly veiled racial epithets. The racist action of the beauty queue seems obvious, but the fact that there is a queue at all is the less obvious but equally damaging effect. So the beauty queue is racist in its hierarchy of women by color and misogynist in its function to objectify all women.

In their 1945 study of Chicago, Drake and Cayton reported discrimination against darker-skinned black women seeking certain types of

employment where beauty mattered.[48] Employers wanted to please customers and anticipated that the best way to do that was to hire "pretty"
black women who, it was assumed, would be light-skinned. In today's job
market, we might consider those jobs where beauty matters to be "front
office appearance" jobs, such as receptionists, administrative assistants,
and hostesses. Also, hiring pretty black or Chicana women may be an
employer strategy to reduce customer resistance to African American
and Mexican American employees in general.

Similar messages about beauty and skin color were prevalent in the
Mexican American community in the 1940s. Many advertising campaigns of major cosmetic companies told Mexican American women,
"'Those with lighter, more healthy skin tones will become much more
successful in business, love, and society'."[49] Advertisements such as these
demonstrate the messages women received about the importance of light
skin and beauty. Both black and Mexican American women often used
chemical products to emulate whiteness. "The popularity of bleaching
creams offers a poignant testament to color consciousness in Mexican
communities, a historical consciousness accentuated by Americanization
through education and popular culture."[50] Color consciousness and the
pursuit of whiteness is the backdrop for contemporary definitions of
beauty and femininity in communities of color.

## CONTROLLING IMAGES OF RACE AND SEXUALITY

Gender and sexuality are important components of racist ideologies
employed against Mexican American and African American women.
Although there are many racial/sexual images of Mexican American
and African American men and women, a few stand out as particularly
related to the violence committed against people of color. I am interested
in how these images of black women and Mexican American women,
usually portrayed as either sexually promiscuous or overly maternal and
pious, invoke skin color (either light or dark) to help communicate their
meanings. Images such as the African American Mammy (usually dark)
and Jezebel (often light), and the Mexican American Catholic mother
(usually light) and "hot tamale" (usually dark) all call many American
characters to mind.[51] Before I discuss any of these controlling images,
I must first discuss the cult of white womanhood, to which all other
racial/sexual images react.

As discussed earlier, the purity of the white race was (and arguably
still is) considered a pressing public issue. In the eyes of white leaders of
the time, the key to maintaining white race purity was the white woman.
If men could control her sexuality and ensure that she only had sexual

relations with white men, then they would be assured of white race purity. The cult of the white woman then, developed into an image of a chaste, pristine, dependent, passive woman.[52] This character became the definition of femininity and womanhood from the times of slavery until the 1960s.

The motivation for violence and terrorism is social control. During the Spanish colonization of California in the 1700s, sexual terrorism was rampant in the small communities there. Spanish soldiers were so exceptionally violent in their treatment of Mexican women, that the entire colonial mission was jeopardized. Mexican men and women resisted control by whites in part because of their shockingly debased and violent behavior toward the women; they were frequently attempting to rape them. In order to justify their own abhorrent behavior, Spanish soldiers there, and in other places, created controlling images of Mexican women as oversexed and whorish to justify their suppression.[53]

Images of Chicanas were created in direct opposition to the cult of white womanhood. Usually portrayed as sexual, debased, and aggressive, these women of color were characterized as the antithesis of white women, and thus the antithesis of the concept of "woman" itself. Some of the early sexualized racist images of Mexican American women focus around the notion of the dark Indian woman as a prostitute or whore.[54] Darker skin color was also a common element of the image of the oversexualized Mexican woman. Mexican women were often portrayed as sexually promiscuous and always sexually available for white and Mexican men.[55] There was also a class element to the racial/sexual images of Chicanas. "Unlike the elite Californio's daughters, however, lower-class Mexican women were rarely viewed and represented in positive terms. In fact, they were derisively portrayed in Anglo travel literature as sexually promiscuous women of ill-repute."[56] From the stereotype of the Gold Rush prostitute, the image of the "hot tamale" Mexican woman evolved. The "hot tamale" has an insatiable sexual appetite and is characterized as la puta, a whore. Taking aspects of the climate and culture of Mexico, whites created an image, through class and color, used to justify sexual violence against Mexican American women. In describing Chicana images in early Western movies, Carlos Cortés writes, "Moreover, in keeping with the filmic pattern of asserting Anglo ethnic superiority, the Anglo hero usually won the light-skinned Mexican woman from a dark-skinned Mexican man, your standard, useful-but-disposable Indianized Mexican greaser."[57] Skin color was an important signifier in Hollywood film, with almost no diversions from the "lighter is better" mantra.

However, the stereotypes were not exclusively over-sexualized images of Chicanas. The Madonna/Whore dualism was invoked with the representation of either virginal pious women or oversexed dancing girls. Jenny Rivera describes the prevalence of the stereotype of the dutiful, Catholic woman who is submissive and traditional. "The Latina is constructed as docile and domestic...She is treasured as a self-sacrificing woman who will always look to the needs of others before her own. The influence of Catholicism throughout Latin America solidifies this image within the community."[58] The two controlling images of Mexican American women as whores (dark) or as Madonnas (light) mirror a similar experience for black women with racial imagery.

The sexual and racial images of African American women as oversexed or whorish is also a direct reaction to the cult of white womanhood. Because black women were deliberately dehumanized, they were denied even a basic identity as women. When enslaved, they were forced to work alongside men in physically strenuous tasks, for long hours. They were not seen as pristine, dependent, passive, fragile, or as having any of the traits that defined white womanhood. Instead, African American women were used as workhorses who were also forced to be always sexually available to white men. Black women were "de-feminized" because they occupied a gendered space for which there was no clear gender identity. They were wives and mothers, but they were also (unlike many white women) workers, independent from men, and strong. This combination of traits left black women in a non-gendered space where they did not have access to the rights of men, nor did they share in the female protections of patriarchy.[59]

Capitalism also has a hand in the creation of these images of women because it was the need for free labor in the Southern capitalist slave economy that structured the roles for black men and women and their images. Capitalism required that black women not be seen as "full women" as white women were in order to maintain the high demands of slave labor and sexual availability for white men.[60] This is another example of how capitalism, in addition to racism and patriarchy, has a hand in structuring the oppression of men and women of color.

Just as the stereotypes of women of color are created in reaction to the myth of white womanhood, so are the stereotypes of men of color. African American men were viewed by whites as the number one threat to white women, and consequently to white nationhood. Whites constructed black men as sexually potent, violent, and lustful of white women and white power. Dark skin and animal-like features were also integral to how this image was created in the press and media, then and now. Cedric Herring reminds us of the darkening of O. J. Simpson on the cover of *Time* magazine to demonstrate the enduring significance of color and criminal images.[61] This characterization served as a rationalization for the frequent lynchings of black men in response to alleged sexual relations with or rapes of white women. Lynching demonstrates the sexualization of racism very well because lynching was often the result of a black man being falsely accused of raping (or even looking at) a white woman.[62] Lynching rose in frequency when black people gained any amount of political or economic power.[63] "White men were willing to engage in the ultimate form of extralegal violence to maintain superiority and dominance, knowing that caste solidarity protected them from trial, conviction, and punishment."[64] This is the origin of the myth of the black rapist. Noted activist and scholar Angela Davis writes, "The myth of the black rapist was a distinctly political invention."[65] The myth of the black male rapist served primarily to socially control and repress African American power, especially in times of economic recession or increasing black civil rights. This myth is not a relic of the past. It is routinely used in popular culture as well as political debates about schooling, crime, and the economy.

By creating black men as monsters, and a threat to white racial purity, via the possibility of sexual relations with white women, whites effectively created an enemy that they could all rally against.[66] "The invocation of the theme of protection of white woman,... surfaces all over the world as the banner to unite the white population and justify violence against the colonized."[67] Further, the threat of potent black male sexuality provides a basis for controlling white women under the guise of "protection." "The Negro became (and still is) the scapegoat of the ideology of sex and racism as it was (and is) accepted by the white woman in southern culture. While she did not actually lynch and castrate Negroes herself, she permitted her men to do so in her name."[68] In this quote, the controversial Calvin Hernton assigns white women some responsibility for the lynchings of African American men. He argues that although they might not have committed the actual act, they participated in a system that gave rise to such racial/sexual violence, embedded themselves in its protections, and enjoyed its privileges. The way that white women were, and still are, constructed in relation to black men and women reveals how the intersections of racism and patriarchy operate to oppress different race/gender groups, with the exception of white men. The glaring absence of white men in any of our negative cultural imagery illustrates how much power they have as a group to control ideological images of others for their own benefit.

Corollary colonial images were created by whites about Mexican

American men. "Lower-class Mexican men generally were seen as libidinally uncontrolled and sexually threatening. The Anglo mind conjured an image of them as 'rapacious' and 'hot-blooded' creatures who wantonly lusted after innocent white women."[69] The similarity between this image of Mexican American men and the image of African American men is striking. Both invoke the image of a low status, dark-skinned man of color trying to use rape/sexual violence as the means to access white power. Historically, men of color are portrayed as villains who try to rape white women and ultimately try to destroy white nationhood.

The image of the rapist was used very directly against Mexican American men in the 1940s. The Zoot Suit Riots have become an infamous part of American history. During this time white Navy soldiers who were docked in Los Angeles roved the streets of East Los Angeles beating Mexican American men as a form of racial terrorism and social control.[70] Frequent justifications for the beatings were false accusations that the Mexican American man had dated or raped (which became synonymous for many whites) a white woman. The racial status of white men protected them from prosecution. Mexican American men were purposefully not protected by the police: They turned a blind eye to the barbaric violence committed by white soldiers against Mexican American men. Again the cult of white womanhood creates in its image a man of color as rapist and serves as a rationale for continued suppression of Mexican people.

One of the tragic contradictions of the sexualized nature of racism is in the myth that all African American men are rapists, and simultaneously, no African American women can be raped. By this, I mean that black men are constructed in the American collective imagination as a potential threat to white race purity and white power. In response to this threat, African American men and boys, must be socially controlled, often through violence and later through incarceration. Conversely, African American women are often constructed as oversexed whores who would never refuse sex and therefore cannot be raped, even by the stereotypic sexually violent black men.

Another effect of the intersection of racism and patriarchy is the conundrum of racism and sexism that black women found themselves in once freed from slavery. Part of the process of dehumanizing black women included denying them the status of "woman," which was at the time defined by the cult of white womanhood: passive, dependent, and chaste. Once black women were freed from bondage, in pursuit of racial liberation they began to insist on being treated as women, treatment they had been denied because of race. During Reconstruction, some African American women left the labor force, and worked only in the home, emulating femininity through the cult of domesticity. However, by asserting their racial freedom in this way, black women were supporting the patriarchal notion of womanhood: a submissive, dependent woman with little autonomy.[71] Black women find themselves in the awkward space of resisting racism and consequently reinforcing patriarchy by trying to attain womanhood in the way it has been defined by white men and women. Bonnie Thornton Dill has referred to the complexity of black women's identities in a white-dominated world as the "dialectics of black womanhood."[72]

There is a similar conundrum for men regarding race and masculinity. One of the ways that African American men have asserted their racial freedom is to wrest control over their families from the hands of whites. During slavery the African American family was entirely disrespected by whites and systematically broken up to reduce the likelihood of rebellions. Whites had near total control over black families and black men (and women) were powerless to stop it. In reaction to their perceived "emasculation," a movement has resulted for black men to take charge of their families and re-establish their own masculinity that was denied them during slavery. Again, this definition of manhood was proffered by whites and in turn, black men's efforts to resist racism reasserted patriarchal power and black women's subjugation in the family.

A similar Catch-22 exists for Mexican American women and men. Mexican American men have traditionally been constructed by whites as being extremely patriarchal and full of *machismo*. Some describe machismo as a form of compensation for feelings of powerlessness in a racist society. In fact, the concept of machismo has been used to blame Mexican American people for their lack of assimilation and upward social mobility.[73] This understanding of machismo has been criticized as a one-dimensional view of Mexican American men that unfairly characterizes them as extremely patriarchal.[74] Mexican men's constructed hypermasculinity has been an alibi for white men and their own patriarchal power. Instead of recognizing the real barriers and discrimination that Chicanos face in social and economic arenas, whites turn to machismo as an explanation for Mexican Americans' lack of mobility. Further, white men and women can divert attention from their own patriarchal attitudes and practices by focusing on the concept of machismo and Chicanos. White men and women point to Mexican men as "the macho ones" thereby absolving white men of their own sexism.

The difficulty for Mexican American women in response to this is that they want to be able to resist the sexism of Mexican American masculinity that does exist without reinforcing the racist Anglo notion that Mexican American men are the quintessential patriarchs.[75] Again, the constraints of racism limit one's choices in dealing with sexism, and vice versa. Mexican American women who spoke out against sexism in the Mexican American community in the 1960s Chicano movements were punished by many Chicano men who had internalized the definition of Mexican American men as "macho."[76] "While some Chicana feminists criticized the myth of machismo used by the dominant society to legitimate racial inequality, others moved beyond this level of analysis to distinguish between the machismo that oppressed both men and women and the sexism in Chicano communities in general, and the Chicano movement in particular, that oppressed Chicana women."[77] Many Mexican American women were also accused of "trying to be white" by standing against sexism in their own communities because feminism was typically viewed as a white bourgeois pastime.[78]

These same issues also existed for African American women in the black nationalist segment of the Civil Rights Movement. Black women reported being characterized as bourgeois, or white, in their pursuit of feminist politics. Also, in the Chicano nationalist and black power movements, many men perceived feminism as a diversion from the real issues of race and capitalism.[79] This limited Mexican American and African American women's options in working against racism and sexism.

Controlling images of women and men reflect power differences among racial/gender groups and often invoke skin color in that process. The sexually dangerous African American and Mexican American men are often characterized as dark-skinned. A clear association is constructed between sexuality and dark skin, exoticizing sex and the dark Other. Additionally, racism and sexism interact to limit women and men's choices in resisting these oppressive systems. Skin tone (both actual and symbolic) is invoked when women of color are disparagingly accused of wanting to be "white" by asserting a feminist agenda in their own communities.

# 3

## LEARNING, EARNING, AND MARRYING MORE

Does the lightness or darkness of a woman's skin color affect her educational attainment, income or even the status of her spouse? Yes, it does and in this chapter I analyze two national survey data sets to explain how. Historical and contemporary research on this topic reveals a persistent advantage for light-skinned African Americans and Mexican Americans in terms of educational attainment, income, residential segregation, mental health, and spousal status, among other variables, as discussed in chapter 2. Building on this work, I examine how skin color operates specifically in the lives of women.[1]

Despite the significant amount of research on skin color stratification, little attention has been paid to how skin color operates uniquely in the lives of women. I contend that light skin works as a form of social capital for women. More specifically, light skin tone is interpreted as beauty, and beauty operates as social capital for women. Women who possess this form of capital (beauty) are able to convert it into economic capital, educational capital, or another form of social capital. My use of the term "social capital," from Bourdieu's "symbolic capital," is also inspired by Dorothy Holland and Margaret Eisenhart's use of the term social capital in their study on beauty and the construction of romance.[2] They argue that young women use their beauty and popularity as capital in attracting boyfriends in a university setting. Drawing on the work of these scholars, I define social capital as a form of prestige related to such things as social status, reputation, and social networks. All of these forms of prestige can be converted into economic or educational capital.

Physical appearance tends to be a more important status characteristic for women than for men, although appearance is becoming increasingly important for men.[3] Women are expected to "look their best" at all times. This cultural norm reinforces the importance that men and women put on a woman's physical attractiveness as a measure of her worth, talent, or ability. For women of color, light skin color is closely associated with beauty. In fact, the connection between the two is so close they are often conflated.

In her study of African American adolescent girls, Maxine Leeds calls the skin color hierarchy of women of color a "pigmentocracy." Leeds found that African American girls were acutely aware of black men's preferences for light-skinned women and therefore felt conflicted about contesting white beauty ideals and at the same time aspiring to them to gain the affections of African American boys. Noted anthropologist Patricia Zavella discusses similar findings in her work.[4] According to Zavella, Chicanas grapple with the same issues of identity, color, and status. The primary difference is that Chicanas often want to avoid looking too *Indio* while African Americans want to avoid looking too African. This type of research demonstrates how the ideology of beauty is used to organize women into a "beauty queue" where skin color, hair texture, and facial features determines how socially desirable a woman is in the marriage or dating market.[5] The importance of beauty extends beyond the competition for men, however. Beauty is still extremely important in the pursuit of other resources including education and personal income. The statistical analysis in this chapter will reveal how skin tone plays a significant role in educational attainment, personal income, and spousal status.

Aside from the empirical studies on skin color and beauty, many scholars have created theories of beauty, color, and status, such as Patricia Hill Collins and Cherríe Moraga. Collins argues that standards of beauty that privilege whiteness can only function by degrading blackness. Identity is relational and those that are defined as beautiful are only defined that way in relation to other women who are defined as ugly. Collins contends that white beauty is based on the racist assumption of black ugliness.[6]

Moraga investigates the construct of white beauty from a cultural perspective. She writes that whiteness operates as a "bleaching" agent that could rob her of her culture, language and Chicana identity.[7] Her own high status as a light-skinned Chicana, *la güera*, was communicated to her not only by whites whom she interacted with, but also by members of her own family who had internalized the norms of white privilege. These authors both describe how through the process of beautifying oneself, which in this context means lightening oneself, a woman may increase her value in the sense that she increases her ability to get a job, get a promotion, further her education, or attract a high-status husband. Additionally, her increase in status is often at the expense of darker-skinned women, whom she must be compared to.

African American and Mexican American women both benefit from the high status of light skin. However, the way that light skin operates in each community and its effects on education, income, and spousal status vary substantially.

## QUANTITATIVE DATA AND METHODS

The data for this chapter come from the National Survey of Black Americans and the National Chicano Survey. Although the data were collected over twenty years ago, these surveys remain the best national samples of African Americans and Mexican Americans that include reliable skin color variables. The three dependent variables in my analyses are years of schooling, personal income, and spouse's years of schooling as a proxy for spousal status. I focus on three primary research hypotheses: (1) light-skinned African American and Mexican American women complete more years of schooling than do their darker counterparts, (2) light-skinned African American and Mexican American women receive higher annual personal earnings than do their darker counterparts, and (3) light-skinned African American and Mexican American women marry higher status men than do their darker counterparts. I use multivariate linear regression analysis to examine these hypotheses.

There are 1,310 African American women and 596 Mexican American women in the data sets. However, to test the third hypothesis I use a subset of 419 married African American women and 366 married Mexican American women. Table 3.1 describes the characteristics of both full samples. The mean years of schooling was nine for Mexican American women and eleven for African American women (see Table 3.1).[8] Mexican American women in this sample had mean personal incomes of $7,625 in 1980, while African American women earned a mean income of $7,521. Spousal status, the third dependent variable, was measured as spouse's years of schooling. Mexican American spouses completed nine years of schooling on average and African American spouses completed ten years on average.

There are also six independent variables in the analysis including skin color, mother and father's education, age, marital status, and urban status. Historically, these variables have proven to be important predictors of status for African Americans and Mexican Americans. Skin color is measured in five categories for each data set: very dark, dark, medium,

**Table 3.1** Descriptive Statistics for Dependent and Independent Variables, NCS and NSBA, 1980

|  | Mexican American Women | African American Women |
|---|---|---|
| Total number of participants | 596 | 1,310 |
| Dependent variables |  |  |
| Respondent education (mean years) | 9 | 11 |
| Personal yearly income (mean) | $7,625 | $7,521 |
| Spouse's education (mean years) | 9 | 10 |
| Independent variables |  |  |
| Skin color |  |  |
| Very dark brown | 6% | 7% |
| Dark brown | 25% | 28% |
| Medium | 34% | 46% |
| Light brown | 21% | 16% |
| Very light brown | 13% | 3% |
| Mother's education (mean years) | 5 | 9 |
| Father's education (mean years) | 5 | 8 |
| Age (mean years) | 40 | 43 |
| Married | 70% | 34% |
| Urban residence | 84% | 79% |
| U.S. born | 67% | NA |
| Mexico born | 33% | NA |
| English facility Mean rating (1–5 scale) | 3 | NA |

light, and very light. Respondents' complexions were rated by trained interviewers who used color palettes to identify respondents' skin color as best fitting into one of the five categories. Almost half of the African American women respondents were identified as having a medium brown complexion, while less than 10 percent of them were identified in each of the extreme categories of very light or very dark. Mexican American women were more evenly dispersed among the five color categories. It is important to note that the skin color labels do not have the same meaning for each ethnic group. "Dark brown" for Mexican Americans is lighter than "dark brown" for African Americans. The color labels are relative to the average skin tone in each community.

Both mother and father's education variables were measured as years of completed formal schooling.[9] African American mothers typically completed nine years of schooling and African American fathers typically completed eight years. For Mexican American mothers the median was five years and for Mexican American fathers the median was four years.[10] Respondents' age was measured in years and was included as a control variable to account for the typical increase and decrease in income over the lifespan. The mean age for African American women in the sample was forty-three and mean age for Mexican American women in the sample was forty. Marital status was also a control variable, included to account for typical differences between married and unmarried women's incomes. Thirty-four percent of African American women and 70 percent of Mexican American women were married. Urban residence was included as an independent variable to control for income and educational differences between rural and urban residents. Seventy-nine percent of African American women and 84 percent of Mexican American women lived in urban areas.

Two additional variables were included in the regression analyses for Mexican American women: nativity and English language facility. These two variables are included in the regression analyses of Mexican American women as control variables to take into account the immigration effects that many people of Mexican descent experience. Sixty-seven percent of the women respondents were born in the United States while 33 percent were born in Mexico. English facility is a five category ordinal variable where 1 represents the least facility with English and 5 represents the most facility with English.

As I show, the data analyses confirm the hypotheses that lighter-skinned women are more privileged than darker-skinned women. The extent of this privilege is not the same in each group and the following discussion will explore how skin color privilege operates for women in the African American and Mexican American communities.

## EDUCATIONAL ATTAINMENT

The first set of regression analyses predicts the educational attainment of Mexican American and African American women. Table 3.2 shows the results of a multivariate regression analysis predicting educational attainment for both groups of women. For African American women, skin color is a statistically significant predictor of education. For every additional gradation of lightness (on the 5-point scale) educational attainment increases by one-third of a year. That means that the lightest woman has more than one entire year of additional education than a darker-skinned woman with similar background characteristics. Several other variables were also important in predicting educational attainment

**TABLE 3.2** Regression Coefficients for Equations Predicting Educational Attainment, Mexican American and African American Women, NCS and NSBA, 1980.

| Variables | Mexican American women | African American women |
|---|---|---|
| Skin color | .281* | .327*** |
| | (.119) | (.084) |
| Age | −.078*** | −.063*** |
| | (.010) | (.005) |
| Married | .094 | .596*** |
| | (.300) | (.160) |
| Mother's education | .248*** | .200*** |
| | (.048) | (.030) |
| Mother's education (unknown) | −.797 | −1.527*** |
| | (.456) | (.20) |
| Father's education | .179*** | .048 |
| | (.045) | (.029) |
| Father's education (unknown) | −.297 | −.359* |
| | (.403) | (.178) |
| Urban residence | .372 | 1.270*** |
| | (.357) | (.188) |
| U.S. born | 2.597*** | |
| | (.289) | |
| English facility | .403*** | |
| | (.123) | |
| N = | 551 | 1,265 |
| R squared = | .47 | .37 |

(NT)* = $p < .05$, , *** = $p < .001$
Standard deviations are in parentheses.

for black women. Not knowing one's mother's education level was a strong predictor of a respondent's own educational attainment, lowering the education level by 1½ years. This supports my contention that a woman is more likely to know her mother's education level if it is higher rather than lower.[11] Also, women who lived in urban or suburban areas completed an additional 1.2 years more of education than women who lived in rural areas.

The regression analysis predicting educational attainment for Mexican American women yielded many similar results to those for African American women. Skin color was also a significant predictor of their educational attainment. For each level of lighter skin color (where 1 is darkest and 5 is lightest) there is a corresponding .28 increase in the number of years of schooling completed. This means that a woman described as very dark brown-skinned will have completed one less year of education than a very light brown woman with similar background characteristics.

Other independent variables were also significant predictors of education. The strongest predictor of education for Mexican American women was country of nativity. Those women who were born in the United States had 2½ years more education on average than those who were born in Mexico, reflecting the fact that average educational levels are higher in the United States than they are in Mexico. This may also be an effect of selective migration where Mexican agricultural migrants are likely to have low levels of formal education. English language facility was also an important predictor of educational attainment for Mexican American women. Those who were one increment more proficient in English (on a 5-point scale) completed 0.4 more years of schooling. This is a very large effect because it means that the most fluent English speakers complete 1½ years more school than those who are least fluent in English. The relationship between these two variables (schooling and English facility) is complicated. The higher the proficiency in English, the more years of schooling, but the more years of schooling one completes, the better one should be at speaking English.

## INCOME

The second hypothesis predicted that lighter-skinned African American and Mexican American women receive higher annual earnings than do darker-skinned women of the same groups. To test this hypothesis, two separate multivariate regression analyses again were conducted. The results of the first regression predicting the personal income of African American women are displayed in Table 3.3. Table 3.3 shows that skin color is a statistically significant predictor of personal income for black women. For every increment of lightness on the color scale, income increases by $673 annually. For instance, an African American woman who is rated as medium brown earns $673 less per year than another woman with similar characteristics who is "light brown." The consequence of this finding is that a woman described as very light brown earns over $2,600 more per year than a woman of similar background who is described as very dark brown.

Parental educational levels did not have a significant effect on respondent income for either racial-ethnic group. However, this finding is consistent with the status attainment literature. Parental education affects respondent education, and respondent education affects respondent income.

**TABLE 3.3.** Regression Coefficients for Equations Predicting Personal Income, Mexican American and African American Women, NCS and NSBA, 1980.

| Variables | Mexican American women | African American women |
|---|---|---|
| Skin color | 57.66 | 673.2* |
| | (156.4) | (295.7) |
| Age | 26.4 | 84.8*** |
| | (16.4) | (17.9) |
| Married | 180.3 | 396.4 |
| | (381.3) | (551.0) |
| Mother's education | 44.6 | 29.45 |
| | (61.7) | (105.0) |
| Mother's education (unknown) | −743.3 | −207.2 |
| | (691.4) | (715.8) |
| Father's education | −23.4 | 155.8 |
| | (56.8) | (99.4) |
| Father's education (unknown) | −156.9 | −1131.0 |
| | (589.5) | (615.1) |
| Urban residence | 119.0 | 2580.47*** |
| | (469.4) | (654.6) |
| Respondent education | 246.2*** | 1183.3*** |
| | (59.0) | (99.0) |
| U.S.born | −461.4 | |
| | (432.9) | |
| English facility | 20.6 | |
| | (165.2) | |
| N = | 302 | 1,134 |
| R squared = | .10 | .19 |

(NT)* = $p < .05$, , *** = $p < .001$
Standard deviations are in parentheses.(ENT)

The other important independent variables for black women were age, urban residence, and education. For each additional year of age, respondents experienced an $84 increase in their annual income. Women who lived in urban or suburban areas received over $2,500 more per year in annual income than did women who lived in rural settings. Lastly, respondent education was a very strong predictor of personal income for African American women. For every additional year of education, women received $1,183 more in annual earnings. Urban residence, age, and education are all typical variables that would affect income. The fact that skin color was also a significant predictor of income attests to its strength in influencing the relationship between human capital and earnings.

The second income regression analysis tests the hypothesis that light-skinned Mexican American women receive higher personal incomes than darker-skinned Mexican American women. While skin color increased income for lighter-skinned women, this effect is not statistically significant. Furthermore, the variables we would expect to be predictors of income such as, urban residence, age, nativity, and English facility, also are not significant.

The only variable that was a significant and direct predictor of Mexican American women's personal income was education. For every additional year of education, a woman would receive $246 more of annual income. This figure is startlingly different from the $1,183 that African American women receive for each additional year of education. One possible explanation suggested by the data is that with so few people graduating from high school, and an average woman's educational attainment of nine years (at the time the data was collected in 1980), there is relatively little variation in educational attainment that could affect income.

These regression analyses reveal different outcomes for Mexican American and African American women. For Mexican American women, skin color has a near zero, direct effect on annual income, even though the skin color coefficient is positive. However, skin color does have an indirect effect on income because, as shown in Table 3.2, it significantly affects educational attainment, and educational attainment is the single strongest predictor of income for Mexican American women. For African American women skin color directly affects income. The lighter a black woman's skin color the more income she receives every year. This finding is consistent with my hypothesis that lighter-skinned women will be rewarded with higher incomes. In summary, it seems that light skin increases income for African American women, but works indirectly on the incomes of Mexican American women.

## SPOUSAL STATUS

The last section of this analysis concerns status negotiation in the marriage market. I hypothesized that lighter-skinned Mexican American and African American women would be more likely to marry high-status men than darker women of those groups. This hypothesis is born out of a theory that suggests that light skin color for women is high status and that marital homogamy prescribes that high-status people are likely to marry one another. Although status may be measured in many ways, I have chosen spousal educational attainment as a proxy for spousal status in this analysis. It is also possible that the practice of hypergamy is at work where individuals marry to move up in social status. In this case, marrying a light-skinned woman may be an opportunity for a man to raise his own status. In either case, light skin color acts as a form of social capital that is either used for an even swap of one high status for another or as a way to "marry up" and increase one's status.[12]

Before analyzing whether or not light-skinned women are more likely to marry high status men than are darker-skinned women, I first establish whether lighter-skinned women are more or less likely to be married at all compared to darker-skinned women. Table 3.4 shows the distribution of marital status and skin color among African American and Mexican American women. It shows that in all categories of skin color about two thirds of Mexican American women were likely to be married at the time of the survey. There are slight quantitative differences among the cells in the table, but a chi square test shows that Mexican American women of all skin colors are equally likely to be married.

A similar analysis was done on African American women and marital status. The most striking difference between the two groups of women is that Mexican American women are much more likely to be married than African American women. About one third of African American women in all skin color groups are married. There is some difference in the exact percentage of African American women married from each skin color category, but a chi square test of significance shows that the African American women of all skin colors are equally likely to be married. This brings the analysis to the next step. If lighter-skinned women in each group are no more likely to be married than darker-skinned women, are lighter-skinned women marrying higher status men than darker-skinned women? The regression analyses in Table 3.5 answer that question.

Table 3.5 shows the results of a regression analysis predicting spouse's level of education for the subset of African American and Mexican American women who are married. In this equation the dependent variable is spousal education and the only independent variables are respondent education, respondent skin color, and mother's education. The other independent variables were dropped from the equation because they are not predictors of, nor control variables for, spousal education.

Among married African American women, all the independent variables have a statistically significant effect on spouse's education. The most important predictor is respondent's own education. For every additional year of education a respondent had, her spouse had an additional .58 years of schooling. This implies that on average black women marry men who are less educated than they are. This is consistent with

**TABLE 3.4.** Percentage Distribution of Mexican American and African American Women by Skin Color and Marital Status, NCS and NSBA, 1980.

|  |  | Very dark | Dark | Medium | Light | Very light | Total |
|---|---|---|---|---|---|---|---|
| Mexican American women | Married | 62 | 67 | 73 | 73 | 72 | 400 |
|  | Single | 38 | 33 | 27 | 27 | 38 |  |
| African American women | Married | 29 | 31 | 37 | 35 | 32 | 439 |
|  | Single | 71 | 69 | 63 | 65 | 67 |  |

*Note*: chi square test shows that cell differences are not statistically significant within ethnic groups.

the literature describing differences in educational attainment between African American women and men.[13] Mother's education also affects the respondent's spouse's education level. Most important for this study, black women's skin color significantly influences her spouse's level of education, as hypothesized. For every increment in light skin color, black

**TABLE 3.5.** Regression Coefficients for Equations Predicting Spouse's Education, Married Mexican American and Married African American Women, NCS and NSBA, 1980.

| Variables | Mexican American women | African American women |
|---|---|---|
| Skin color | −.052 | .287* |
|  | (.170) | (.148) |
| Respondent education | .623*** | .581*** |
|  | (.059) | (.047) |
| Mother's education | −.094 | .142** |
|  | (.056) | (.047) |
| Mother's education (unknown) | −1.250* | −.766** |
|  | (.585) | (.300) |
| U.S. born | −.165 |  |
|  | (.431) |  |
| English facility | .437** |  |
|  | (.172) |  |
| N = | 366 | 419 |
| R squared = | .40 | .41 |

(NT)* = $p < .05$, ** = $p < .01$, *** = $p < .001$.
Standard deviations are in parentheses.

women's spouses complete another .28 years of school. That means that when a very dark brown woman and a very light brown woman who are similar in background characteristics marry, the very light brown woman will likely marry a man with an entire year of more education than the very dark brown woman. This finding suggests that light skin is a valuable commodity for women allowing them greater access to high-status, well-educated spouses.

Table 3.5 shows a similar regression for a married subset of Mexican American women. In this regression, the same independent variables were included with the addition of nativity and English facility. This analysis shows that the skin color of a Mexican American woman does not significantly affect her choice of marriage partners. This is a surprising result and contrary to my hypothesis. It is possible that light-skinned Mexican American women are still privileged in the marriage market, but for other reasons, such as a lack of sufficient educational diversity among Mexican American men, the pattern is not strong enough to be revealed in a regression analysis. I explore this possibility further in the discussion section.

Other independent variables in this regression also are significant predictors of spouse's education. The variable, "don't know mother's education," was a statistically significant predictor of spouse's education, as was a woman's education and English facility. In fact, the respondent's education was the strongest predictor of her spouse's education. For each year increase in a married Mexican American woman's education, there was a corresponding .62 increase in her husband's education. Again, this suggests that Mexican American women have higher levels of educational attainment than Mexican American men. Finally, a woman's level of English facility had a great impact on the education of her spouse. For every additional level of her English facility (on a 5-point scale) her husband had an additional .44 years of schooling.

## PATTERNS OF PRIVILEGE

This analysis has shown that skin color does indeed affect major life outcomes for African American and Mexican American women. As predicted, light skin bestows privileges in education and income for both groups, and even higher spousal status for African American women. How does this process of privilege occur?

In order to make sense of any racialized process, it is imperative to examine the intertwined history of the groups at issue. As discussed in chapter 2, African Americans and Mexican Americans had histories of slavery and colonization, as well as contemporary racial oppression and discrimination. Whites assigned meanings to whiteness, blackness, and brownness that valued them each differently. As an abstract concept, whiteness is believed to represent civility, intelligence, and beauty, and in contrast, blackness and brownness are seen as representing primitiveness, ignorance, and ugliness. These abstract concepts took on representations in the form of actual physical traits associated with each racial group. This is an example of a racial project. Racial projects are campaigns to establish the meaning and construction of race in any given time period. Racial projects establish what "race" means historically through images, representations, and explanations about racial categories or groups.

In the case of Mexican Americans, dark skin signifies ignorance, laziness, and provincial ways.[14] These racial meanings are rooted in Spanish colonialism and American imperialism. Racial projects have constructed African Americans as dangerous, angry, incompetent, and over-sexual. My analysis shows how society disperses resources in accordance with its racial meanings. African American and Mexican American women with dark brown skin (and ethnic features) receive fewer rewards in society, even when they invest the same amount of human capital as those with lighter skin. African American and Mexican American women who more closely resemble whites receive more rewards, even when they do not work or study harder than their darker-skinned sisters. This is the essence of skin color stratification. Racism and colorism operate on a daily basis as individuals evaluate others based on their physical characteristics. Phenotype mediates the way people are perceived. Seeing some facial features negatively and others positively, and the consequential valuation of lightness over darkness, is the mechanism through which contemporary skin color stratification occurs in the United States.

As shown in the regression analyses, educational attainment is one of the most significant predictors of income for people in the United States. Therefore, it is imperative that all people have the same ability to take advantage of educational opportunities. By combining the results of Tables 3.2 and 3.3, we see that education mediates the effects of skin color on income. We can assume it works at many levels including the self, the family, schools, and other institutions. Unfortunately, all of these levels of expectations are affected by a pervasive racist ideology. White teachers and administrators are prone to make distinctions among African American and Mexican American children about who the "smart kids" are and who the "good kids" are. Those distinctions are often influenced by our cultural standard of racism. Consequently, the African American child with curly light brown hair and the Mexican American child with blonde hair and green eyes may be identified as the smarter kids. Those who most closely resemble whites may have more so-called white traits attributed to them such as intelligence and civility. This is very important as teachers interact with students and reward those they think are the smartest and the best. If some lighter-skinned children have one white parent they may have access to structural privileges associated with whiteness, such as economic capital or social networks, in addition to symbolic ones.

Light skin also provides an advantage in income attainment. Lighter-skinned black women are more likely to earn high wages than their darker-skinned sisters with similar credentials. This is a particularly significant finding for women since physical appearance is an important commodity for them in the labor force. Skin color is integral to the definition of beauty; light skin is equated with attractiveness. Because of the greater importance of physical appearance for women, skin color matters more for women. Color can mediate negotiations for obtaining jobs, getting promotions and raises, and as we already saw, even getting an education. Because light skin is associated with competence and whiteness, light skin is more desirable by white employers and employers of color who have internalized white racial hierarchies.

These findings corroborate those by Maxine Thompson and Verna Keith in their study of skin tone, income, and self-esteem. They found that lighter-skinned African American women have higher levels of self-esteem than darker-skinned women. However, for women with the highest income levels, self-esteem is not predicted by color.[15] Their research adds yet another dimension to the matrix of color, status, beauty, and income.

The last set of analyses that dealt with spousal status showed varying results between the two groups of women. Light-skinned African American women had a clear advantage in the marriage market and were more likely to marry high status men than were darker-skinned women. This finding is consistent with the other findings on color and life chances, where light skin is always privileged. This is also consistent with popular understandings within the black community about beauty and status. The popular media has frequently taken up the issue of colorism and dating in the African American community with countless articles in black magazines, and even books and movies dedicated to the topic.[16] Perhaps this is the most disturbing finding because skin color's effect on the marriage market is something that is internal to the black community. Whites have a significant role in maintaining skin color stratification in terms of income and education, as they are the majority of employers and educators. But they are not the majority of marriage partners for African American women, so skin color hierarchies in the marriage market suggest the pervasiveness of racist ideologies that value whiteness and emulations of it.

This may also be true for Mexican American women, but the results are less certain. The regression analysis showed that skin color did not significantly affect the educational status of spouses for Mexican American women. This is curious because it is inconsistent with the other findings on the privilege of light skin and also because it is at odds with the prevailing preference within the Mexican American community for light-skinned women, or *las güeras*. My results may show that skin color privilege is not as entrenched in the status system of the Mexican American community as it is in the African American community. Another possibility is that there is not enough variation in the educational levels of the Mexican American spouses in the sample precluding any correlation between educational attainment and skin color of women. Whatever the exact reason for this finding, light skin does not seem to offer a significant privilege for Mexican American women in marrying high-status husbands in this data set.

The analysis of quantitative survey data has shown that in the areas of education, personal income, and spousal status, skin color mediates outcomes and advantages for the light-skinned. I suggest that this happens in large part because racial ideologies devalue the phenotypes of African Americans and Mexican Americans and associate their features with ignorance and ugliness. Further, because physical appearance matters more for women in terms of access to resources (income and education), skin color matters more for women and stratifies them in many areas of life. European colonization and slavery have left a lasting imprint on African American and Mexican American women through the skin color hierarchies that privilege light skin over dark skin.

# 4

## BLACK AND BROWN BODIES
## UNDER THE KNIFE

My parents always taught me to be proud of my black skin, but when I was home recently, I was watching my mom put on her makeup and she drew the lipstick way up in the middle of her lip. And I said, 'Why aren't you filling in your lip?' And she said, 'Well, I don't want my lips to look big.' And I was like, 'This is so ironic because you have always said, 'the blacker the berry, the sweeter the juice' and 'be proud.'' And she was drawing in her lips halfway![1]

Kitara's description of her mom's struggle between black pride and her own African features is emblematic of that experienced by many people of color. Despite the social movements of the 1960s and 1970s that proclaimed "black is beautiful" and "brown pride," many blacks and Chicano/as still harbor shame about typically ethnic characteristics such as full lips, or broad, flat noses. And just as skin color matters for access to resources, so do facial features.

Anglo facial features are generally viewed as high status argue Arce, Murguia, and Frisbie in their 1980 study of Chicanos in the United States. They found that Anglo features, especially when combined with light skin color, provided a substantial boost in status for Mexican Americans.[2] This finding is true among the affluent in Mexico as well. In fact, so many young women, and even men, are concerned about attaining Anglo features that Mexico has the highest level of teenage plastic surgery in the world. Over one-fourth of all cosmetic surgery patients in Mexico are teenagers. In 2002, *The Mirror* printed a story on Luccianna Ordaz Balderas, a beautiful and rich 12-year-old girl in Mexico City.

> "I hate my nose," she says… "I'd like a Britney Spears or Kirsten Dunst nose. They have more delicate features than Mexican women." Luccianna isn't unusual. Each year, thousands of young Mexicans between 12 and 25 go under the knife in pursuit of perfection.[3]

Luccianna's desire to have a nose like Britney Spears or Kirsten Dunst speaks volumes about the politics of race, ethnicity, and the body. Nose surgeries routinely creating less indigenous and more Anglo noses have become mainstream among elite teenagers in Mexico. The pursuit of high-status facial features is the focus of this chapter.

Facial features have long been considered in much the same way skin color has: the whiter the better. Mexican Americans or African Americans with longer, narrower noses are often told that they are lucky to have such a "good nose." Lips have been a point of contention among African Americans, as well. Only slightly full lips are most desirable whereas larger, fuller lips are frequently made fun of and identified as "African" features and considered low status. Eye color is also an important indicator of ethnic identity and social status. Light colored eyes, such as blue or green, are very highly valued in African American and Mexican American communities. These serve as only a few examples of the importance of facial features in communicating status in the United States.[4]

Although skin color has proven hard to change, despite an internationally booming skin bleaching industry, it has become much easier and more acceptable to change facial features through the use of cosmetic surgery. With a growing middle class and advanced technologies that reduce keloid scarring on darker skin tones, more and more people of color are purchasing facial cosmetic surgeries.[5] Once considered only appropriate or necessary for celebrities, the number of cosmetic procedures[6] has astronomically increased among middle-class Americans. Although there are many interesting angles from which to discuss the growing number of cosmetic procedures, this chapter will focus on the racial motivations and outcomes of this growing trend. Just as skin color is a form of social capital, Anglo facial features provide a similar kind of social capital that can be used to gain esteem in employment, education, community, and the marriage market. As one of the African American women I interviewed suggested, "If you're really dark and you have African features you probably will have problems in this society with dating or people thinking you're good looking, because it's hard." It is this reality that is often publicly denied but privately acknowledged that has motivated thousands of African Americans and Mexican Americans to go under the knife.

At first glance, it would seem that people of color are significantly less interested in cosmetic surgery than whites. Data from 2002 indicate that whites make up 81 percent of purchasers of cosmetic procedures, slightly more than their representation in the U.S. population, while Latinos make up 8 percent, African Americans 5 percent, and Asians 4 percent.[7] These statistics reveal slight over-representations for whites and under-representations for Latinos and African Americans. Moreover, when polled, people of color expressed less interest in choosing cosmetic surgery for themselves in the future than did whites.[8] From these data it seems that for whatever reason (cultural, religious, or economic) Latinos and African Americans are less interested in the cosmetic alteration of their bodies. Further analysis reveals this could not be farther from the truth.

In fact, African Americans and Latinos are flocking to cosmetic surgeons in staggering numbers as never seen before. Between 1999 and 2001 the number of whites who purchased a facial cosmetic or reconstructive procedure increased by 34 percent. By contrast, there was a 200 percent increase among Latino patients and an over 300 percent increase for African Americans and Asian Americans.[9] The overall numbers of blacks and Latinos purchasing cosmetic procedures (5 percent and 8 percent respectively) hide the rapidly growing trends within each of these groups to purchase more facial cosmetic procedures every year. The number of cosmetic procedures completed in the United States has steadily increased every year since the late 1980s.[10] By 1997, 2.1 million cosmetic procedures were performed. And by 2002, a whopping 6.9 million cosmetic procedures were performed, 88% of which were performed on women.[11]

Currently, the most common surgeries performed on women today are liposuction, breast augmentations, eyelid surgeries, nose surgeries, and breast reductions.[12] These top five procedures tell us some interesting things about women and their feelings about their bodies. Not surprisingly, two of the top five procedures women choose involve breasts. Either making them bigger (a more common choice) or making them smaller, women's breasts continue to be a body part in need of alteration. Just as interesting as the focus on breasts, however, is the focus on facial characteristics—particularly those that are often associated with ethnic identity. Two of the top five procedures for women are alterations to the face: eyelid surgery and nose surgery. Although sometimes done for other reasons, women often choose to have these facial features altered in order to achieve a more Anglo appearance.[13] Thousands of Asian and Asian American women, and growing numbers of men, pay for eyelid surgeries that add a crease to their eyelids to give them a more rounded appearance—more Western. In addition, many women of color: Latinas, African Americans, and Asian Americans purchase nose surgeries that make their noses longer or narrower—more Anglo. In 2002 African American plastic surgery patients opted to have their noses reconstructed at almost twice the rate of white plastic surgery patients.[14] The top five cosmetic surgeries chosen by women in the United States reflect not only the gendered concern with breast size and shape, but also the racial concerns about facial features and beauty.

How can we make sense of the growing trend of cosmetic surgery in relation to people of color? Is cosmetic surgery a "free choice" or a "coercive racial corrective?" I propose a theory from Kathryn Pauly Morgan to begin the analysis. In her essay "Women and the Knife: Cosmetic Surgery and the Colonization of Women's Bodies" Morgan argues that the discourse around cosmetic surgery is constructed in such a way as to obscure its actual dominating influence.[15] She argues that there are three "paradoxes" of cosmetic surgery that are crucial to its insidious influence. First, cosmetic surgery is discursively constructed as a "free choice" suitable to an individual woman's particular preferences. Many surgeons and advertisements promise to help women achieve their own "personal goals" or "individual beauty." In fact, Morgan argues, cosmetic surgery is a choice of conformity. Whether one chooses a breast augmentation, nose job, tummy tuck, eyelid surgery, or liposuction, all of these choices lead to a similar physical appearance: namely "White, Western, Anglo Saxon bodies."[16] Morgan's second paradox exposes the myth of surgery as liberation. Many people construct cosmetic surgery as a liberating tool for women where they are free to create their bodies as they want them. In an inversion of more mainstream feminist arguments, some postmodern scholars have argued that cosmetic surgeries allow women the power to define their bodies and thus themselves in any way they want—giving them the ultimate freedom. Actually, Morgan suggests, cosmetic surgery is a colonization of the body. It is not freedom at all, but the exact opposite, domination. Cosmetic surgeries alter women's bodies for the public gaze. Instead of women creating their bodies for themselves, their own identities or sexuality, cosmetic surgeons re-create the female body for the gaze of an outsider. Third, Morgan argues that the choice of cosmetic surgery is presented as completely voluntary. Women can choose whether or not to have procedures done, and which ones they want. However, cosmetic alteration to the female body has become so pervasive, that many women feel extreme pressure to have the procedures—either to become more beautiful and keep up with the proverbial Joneses, or to "reverse" the effects of aging. There is a coercive element of the U.S. beauty culture that makes cosmetic procedures an imperative, and not a voluntary act at all. In this chapter, I build on Morgan's model of identifying paradoxes and apply it to this investigation of cosmetic surgery and race.

## PARADOX #1: THE NEW GLOBAL BEAUTY

According to mainstream news publications like *Newsweek* and cosmetic industry insiders, there is a new game in town—the new global beauty. Official discourses created both inside and outside of the cosmetic surgery industry are selling the public on a new image: the multicultural beauty. Many surgeons and cosmetic surgery publications tell us that the "old" standard of beauty (read: white and Western) is a thing of the past. It has been replaced with a "new" global or multicultural standard of beauty that appreciates a variety of "ethnic" features. This sounds like good news for women of color, especially considering the strong effect beauty has as a form of social capital. Cosmetic surgery does not make all women look the same, the professionals argue, but it helps each individual woman achieve the best look for her "ethnic" community. This argument was best articulated in the *Newsweek* article "The Global Makeover" published in 2003.[17] In this article, the author argues that supermodel Saira Mohan is the example par excellence of the new global beauty. Her Punjabi Indian and European Canadian background is presented as evidence of the global aesthetic that is now more desirable than previous Western-based models. "She's one of those beautiful women who can easily be Italian, British, or Spanish," fashion photographer Atul Kasekbar is quoted as saying.[18] In defense of her multicultural appeal Kasekbar adds, "And she can very well be an Indian in a sari."[19] In fact, Mohan looks largely white. The paradox of purporting global beauty to a woman who could be mistaken as European, European, or European seems an obvious contradiction. But this is the paradoxical discourse of the new beauty regime. It is simultaneously inclusive, multicultural, and new, while remaining exclusive, Eurocentric, and old. The new global beauty, as Mohan is called in the article, is, in fact, old-fashioned, white beauty repackaged with dark hair. This means that beauty, and thus capital, is still elusive for many women of color as it continues to be defined by primarily Anglo bodies and faces.

Additionally, it is not clear that a new global beauty is truly desirable in a context of neo-colonialism and globalization. Moving toward the Brazilian example, for instance, of exoticizing light brown-skinned *mulatta* women who are dark, and thus sexual, but not too dark and thus not too African or Indian, is a troubling alternative discourse. The exoticization of the light brown woman is not a new global beauty but an old colonial concubine whom one can lust after, but not marry. In fact, it is this image that fuels the growing sex tourism around the globe that commodifies brown women's bodies.

In addition to suggesting that old beauty standards have changed to new ones, other publications from the cosmetic surgery industry have argued in the language of multiculturalism that one defining beauty standard no longer exists. There are now multiple beauty standards—at least one for each culture, they argue. As an appeal to the growing market of people of color choosing cosmetic surgery, industry publications claim, "our culture and the media recognize that the ideal beauty is no longer just the tall, Nordic, blue-eyed blonde. Now ethnic individuals feel they can improve their appearance through cosmetic surgery without having to change to a standard of beauty that doesn't fit them."[20] This cosmetic surgeon argues that there are multiple beauty standards including those that celebrate beauty in various ethnic groups. He suggests that people of color who choose cosmetic surgery procedures are not trying to achieve a white standard of beauty, but rather a standard that is organic to their own communities. The paradox here is that the procedures that black and Latina women choose change their features in patterned ways that mimic white or Anglo faces.

An African American patient described her decision to have a lip reduction as having nothing to do with her ethnic identity. "I'm proud of my heritage. I just wanted to look better and feel more confident about my appearance."[21] This statement is emblematic of the discourse of patients of color because it de-racializes bodies so that lip size has no meaning or status in relation to race. There are simply better lips and worse lips whose racial designations remain invisible. The author of this article, presumably because it is an industry publication, never questions the meaning of the patient's assertion that smaller lips look better.

Another claim made by surgeons is that cosmetic surgeries can actually *enhance* ethnic identity. "Facial plastic surgery was once strictly the realm of Caucasian patients but today is a growing trend among minorities, who seek to enhance rather than shed their ethnicity."[22] The American Society for Aesthetic Plastic Surgery said in a statement that, "cosmetic plastic surgeons now have the knowledge and techniques to help patients preserve their ethnic identity."[23] These claims, which are rampant throughout the literature, turn on its head the argument that cosmetic surgery patients are all trying to be white. What does it mean to enhance ethnic features? Critics wonder if enhancing ethnic features means that patients of color are choosing to have their noses flattened or widened, or if African Americans are seeking to have their lips made larger. In fact, it seems that the opposite is the case. African Americans and Latinos routinely have their noses made longer and narrower, African Americans have their lips reduced, and Asians request their eyes be made rounder and with a crease in the eyelid. All of these procedures seem to move patients of color away from enhancing African, Indian, or Asian ethnic features, and instead toward minimizing them. The industry makes these claims however, because it is tapping into the fear that patients of color have that they will be losing or devaluing their own ethnic identities by choosing cosmetic alteration. The industry publications assure them that they are not trying to be white, and that in fact, they are enhancing their ethnic identity.

## PARADOX #2: WHITE INVISIBILITY
## AND ETHNIC DEFICIENCY

Publications in the cosmetic surgery industry consistently refer to the facial features of people of color as ethnic while never doing the same for whites; white features are always described as normal or in normative terms. This practice has several implications. First, white racial identity is invisible when it is not named. People of color do not have to fear trying to be white, because white features are not specifically labeled as such. People of color just want more "normal" noses and eyes, not a different race's nose or eyes. This also distracts from the fact that everyone, including whites, seems to want whiter features. Because white features are considered normal or average, it seems that everyone is pursuing an aesthetic that has no racial status or implications. In fact, the term normal is quite deceptive. Anglo or white features are not normal at all. They are idealized features. People do not pay thousands of dollars and endure pain and discomfort to look normal—they do it to look ideal. By using the word "normal" to describe highly desirable features, both doctors and patients obscure the reality that white facial features are anything but normal; they are regarded as superior.

The booming business of "fixing" ethnic features so that they are more Anglo, or white, could not thrive if it were not for a discourse that pathologizes people of color's ethnic features as weak, lacking, and inadequate. Eugenia Kaw makes this point in her study of Asian American eyelid surgeries. She says that by using words such as "without," "lack," "sleepy," and "dull" to characterize Asian features, cosmetic surgeons create and perpetuate ideological racism, and thus notions of Asian inferiority.[24] This practice is found throughout the field of cosmetic surgery. Steven Hoefflin in his book *Ethnic Rhinoplasty,* refers more than once to cosmetic surgeons as "sculptors" while referring to African American, Asian, and Latino body parts as "weak," "flat," "deficient," and "challenging."[25] In the publication *Ethnic Considerations in Facial Aesthetic Surgery,* Oscar Ramirez refers to Latino bodies as "depressed," "insufficient," "small," and "retracted."[26] This use of language reinforces the view of white bodies as not only normal, but as most desirable, and all other bodies as inadequate, pathological, and in need of intervention by comparison.

In fact, Hoefflin seems to describe the social position of racial groups through their noses. "Within the three ethnic/racial types considered here (Asian, black, and Hispanic), the Asian nose lies somewhere between the black and Caucasian nose."[27] Asian Americans are "middleman minorities" not just in American cities as owners of small groceries and liquor stores, but apparently also when it comes to facial features. Using a critical discourse analysis in this way reveals how deeply the current racial ideologies of the United States are embedded in the talk of the doctors and publicists of the cosmetic surgery industry.

In a similar vein, Ramirez warns the reader to take special care when surgically altering the eyes of Hispanic patients. "Hispanic patients are very sensitive to changes in the eyelid slant... Hispanic patients are very sensitive about 'Orientalization' of their eye expression. Extreme caution should be taken when planning eyelid and peri-orbital surgery."[28] The social position of different ethnic groups is reflected in the concerns of the cosmetic surgery community. If Latinos are coming in to upgrade their social status by getting more Anglo features, the surgeon must be careful not to inadvertently downgrade their status by making them look more Asian. The serious status concerns around racial and ethnic identity are not lost on the surgeons and researchers in the field. The overt descriptions of the relative status of racialized facial features reveals that beauty is indeed, capital. Even if patients are unwilling to characterize their desires as looking more Anglo, surgeons know that racial status matters to patients and they discuss it in their textbooks and manuals.

## PARADOX #3: I DON'T WANT TO BE WHITE...
## I JUST WANT A WHITER NOSE

When asked about cosmetic surgery by researchers or by doctors, people of color routinely say that they do not want to be white and are not trying to Anglicize their features. However, the cosmetic procedures that people of color choose almost uniformly have the effect of Anglicizing their faces. Asian women rarely, if ever, choose to make their eyes narrower or remove eyelid folds that already exist. Latinas and African Americans almost never choose to make their noses flatter or wider. The Anglo conformity in the shaping of facial features buttresses up against the clear statements made by patients of color that they are not trying to look whiter. This seeming impasse can best be reconciled by taking a more critical look at contemporary racial politics and the norms of beauty.

Strong ingroup norms exist in most communities of color that encourage racial or ethnic pride. In fact, researchers have found that most African Americans think it is inappropriate to favor light skin and express "no preference" when asked about the skin color of an ideal mate.[29] People of color are largely proud to be members of their own ethnic groups and do not generally report that they wish to be white. Despite the attitudes recorded in several studies, researchers have found that light skin still accrues distinct advantages over dark.[30] At the same time, beauty has become so normalized that it now no longer seems social, political, or racial in nature. The discourse on beauty has become mainstreamed such that beauty itself seems natural and outside of the world of culture, politics, and power. The colorblind ideology that has taken a stronghold among Americans today helps explain the reduction in racial awareness, or at least reluctance to name racism when people see it. Our purported colorblindness makes it possible for someone to simply want to be "pretty" and not see that as any indication or contradiction of the strength of her ethnic identity. Sara Goering writes, "Thus, individuals who partake in cosmetic surgery to erase the phenotypic signs of race often claim simply to be attempting to become normal or beautiful."[31] The days of the black Civil Rights Movement, when "black is beautiful" was a popular slogan, seem long gone as critical discussions of beauty and racial aesthetics are now dismissed as incongruent with the values of "personal freedom" and "individual choice."

This sentiment is captured in the magazine *Facial Plastic Surgery Today* in its 1996 article "Facial Plastic Surgery Enhances Ethnic Features." In describing patients of color, the article reads, "Just a generation ago, many of these individuals would have hesitated to seek facial plastic surgery, feeling that to change their physical appearance would in some way be a rejection of their ethnic heritage. No more. Members of minority groups are realizing that the desire to look one's best is a universal one, transcending cultural and racial boundaries."[32] Many now consider beauty, not an artifact of culture, but as a universal truth and therefore outside of the realm of racial power. Both men and women are now encouraged to pursue "universal" beauty or "multicultural" beauty, both euphemisms for the still-dominant white beauty, although beauty still has a much stronger effect on women's status than it does on men's. The quote above suggests, at best, that people of color have finally "realized" that race does not matter in the way it once did, and at worst, that race never really mattered at all.

Downplaying the significance of race is an elaborate ritual in this industry. Silence is used strategically by doctors, patients, and publicists. Patients insist that they are proud to be Latina, or African American, or Asian, while surgeons assure them that their new faces will fix their troubling body parts but maintain their ethnic identities. Neither patient nor surgeon (nor advertisement) ever betrays the racial reality: Anglo facial features reap higher rewards both professionally and personally. No one states the obvious in this industry: that looking whiter is a pathway to higher rewards in a racist society. Because no one is willing to say this out loud, speakers for the industry go through elaborate discursive manipulations to suggest that Anglicizing facial features just makes people look more normal or that their ethnic features are enhanced. Suzanne Fraser found support for this trend in her book *Cosmetic Surgery, Gender, and Culture*, where she analyzed the content of women's magazines. "The bodies represented in the material are overwhelmingly Caucasian, and the procedures, some of which are utilized to modify racial markers such as noses and eyes, are consistently represented as simply about 'beauty'. Evidently, while it is culturally acceptable in women's magazines to experience dissatisfaction with oneself in terms of beauty, and to act on this dissatisfaction to alter aspects of the body and so the self, it is almost taboo to present race in a similar way."[33] Fraser has aptly described not only women's magazines, but also cosmetic surgery industry publications. It is not culturally acceptable, particularly in the United States, for an individual to express dissatisfaction with her racial body and seek to cosmetically alter it. Therefore, this racial dissatisfaction, which must exist in a racist society, gets suppressed and rearticulated as a quest for a normal body.

Despite the deafening silence around racial issues in the cosmetic surgery industry, industry professionals know that patients of color are afraid of being perceived as wanting to be white or are afraid that they actually do want to be white. This is best evidenced in the introduction to Jan Adams' book *Everything Women of Color Should Know About Cosmetic Surgery*. Adams, who is African American, tackles this fear on the first page of the first chapter of his book and wastes no time assuring women of color that they are in no way revealing any private need to be white by purchasing cosmetic procedures. "Psychologists and psychiatrists, along with racial bigots on both sides of the fence, have often attempted to equate a woman's desire for physical improvement through cosmetic surgery with some psychopathological condition akin to self-mutilation."[34] Adams implies that raising the concern that women of color seeking certain kinds of cosmetic surgeries are victims of internalized racism is racist in and of itself. This reversal of meaning is consistent with the dominant U.S. discourse on race in which any talk about race, including racial inequality or racial domination, is seen as racist. This discursive maneuver is a strategy to silence dissent and inquiry about current racial policies and practices.

Despite the fact that there seem to be clear contradictions about the goals, and perhaps motivations, of cosmetic surgeries that Anglicize the facial features of people of color, it is important to point out that I do not believe that patients of color do want to be white, per se. Although much of the evidence points to a clear pattern of changing faces to be whiter, not blacker or browner, beauty has become so entrenched in our daily doses of popular culture, that many people who choose these procedures are not individually troubled or experiencing actual identity crises. It is much more insidious than that. Our entire cultural ethos in the contemporary United States seethes of white beauty. White beauty is normal beauty and white beauty is ideal beauty. Our culture teaches us that beauty matters more for women than almost anything else. The pursuit of beauty is a capital investment for women and the pursuit of white beauty, the only real beauty there is in the United States is doubly so for women of color. This is a very important point. It would be condescending and insulting to suggest that all people of color who choose to purchase cosmetic surgeries are doing so because they want to be white, but it is not egregious to suggest that the choices people make about cosmetic surgery are strongly influenced by our cultural norms of beauty, all of which are white because we live in a context of white racism.

## PARADOX #4: THE PURSUIT OF BEAUTY IS NATURAL/CORRUPT

Publications from the cosmetic surgery industry and related pundits vacillate between opposite but related discourses on beauty: The pursuit of beauty is natural and evolutionary, versus the pursuit of beauty is an unfortunate reality of our corrupt human world. The power of both of these discourses is that they ultimately make the pursuit of beauty an unchangeable aspect of society, and consequently make cosmetic surgery an inevitability.

First, I will describe the beauty is natural and evolutionary discourse. Adams argues that there is a "universal truth that most people make sacrifices in order to appear attractive and desirable. Adorning ourselves with paint, tattoos, scars, jewelry, unnatural hairstyles, or uncomfortable clothing dates from antiquity."[35] This is the naturalized explanation as exemplified by Adams, but also widely used by other writers both inside and outside of the cosmetic surgery profession. Here, the meaning conveyed is that the pursuit of beauty is natural and timeless: it transcends race, gender, colonialism, etc. In this way, it cannot be critiqued or reigned in. Also interesting in the above quote from Adams is his reference to many body practices by people of color such as scarring and painting. By casting rhinoplasties and breast enlargements as something akin to what the ancestors did in the homeland makes the cosmetic surgery process less Anglicizing and threatening to the women of color his book targets.

Other writers, both feminist and not, also describe today's quest for beauty as natural and timeless. In countless magazine articles, the pursuit of beauty is described as a natural, anthropological phenomenon that assures ideal mate selection. Darwin's theory of the survival of the fittest is often invoked in these discussions, including in the title of Nancy Etcoff's book on the topic called *The Survival of the Prettiest*. In it she argues that the pursuit of beauty is not only natural, it is also rational, given the significant power it garners women in today's society.[36]

The flip side of the naturalizing discourse describes the pursuit of beauty as unfortunate, but inescapable in our corrupted, human world. "It's all very nice to say you shouldn't judge a book by its cover, that it is the content that's important. But that's not the way the world works."[37] If he has not yet convinced his reader with the naturalized beauty discourse, Adams then changes direction and enlists the "it's the corrupt reality" discourse. Also popular in the mainstream press, this way of characterizing the problem argues that people judge others by appearance all the time and those who are considered physically attractive gain all kinds of benefits, therefore, we'd all better jump on the bandwagon and deal with the unfortunate, but current reality, and invest in our beauty quotients. Dieting, makeup, and even cosmetic surgeries are all seen as legitimate investments in this discourse. The problem with both of these discourses on beauty is that they lead to the same conclusion, everyone should continue to engage in significant investments in their beauty, including by purchasing cosmetic surgeries. The pursuit of beauty has an air of inevitability in both of these discourses, which leaves no room for critique or social change. Whether one thinks the zeal to acquire beauty is a natural tool of evolution or a corrupt societal reality, these discourses present the pursuit of beauty as a permanent feature of society.

## PARADOX #5: BLACK AND BROWN BEAUTIES: NOW YOU SEE THEM, NOW YOU DON'T

With the barrage of beauty images the average consumer sees in a day, few people have time to critically analyze and reflect on the actual meaning and content of these messages. Despite that, images of women of color in the media have been a frequent point of contention between image-makers and consumers over the years. People of color were largely absent from mainstream media for generations, or only shown in a limited number of degrading roles. Since the Civil Rights Movement, however, more African Americans appear in film, television, and advertisements of all types. People of color are now used to sell products to a general multiracial audience in a way that was unheard of a generation ago.[38] Latinos have only recently begun to be reflected in the media, but are a quickly growing media resource and audience.[39]

Many people of color argue that our media are making progress by including more images of different ethnic groups, particularly in relation to selling beauty products. White women are no longer the only ones selling soap, lotion, and cosmetics. Most of the major cosmetics companies now offer a set of top models representing many races and ethnicities to sell their products. Revlon provides one example. In a series of ads marketed in many magazines, Revlon features a multicultural group of women, including many celebrities, all looking beautiful in Revlon makeup. Is this the solution to the beauty queue? Will more inclusion lead to broader definitions of beauty that appreciate the many ethnic features of women in the United States and around the world? Although many cosmetics companies now also hire women of color, such as Halle Berry and Salma Hayek, to help sell their products, most of these models are light-skinned with Anglo features. This reinforces the same problematic definition of beauty that is already in place, the whiter the better, even for women of color.

The problem with this trend is that the inclusion of women of color into higher profile media outlets as images of beauty can lull women into accepting the ideology of beauty itself as long as it seems inclusive. The controlling ideology of beauty, which commodifies women for an external gaze, is more palatable to all women when it feigns fairness by including a few token women of color. The problem is, the women of color who are included are usually depicted in ways that highlight white forms of beauty. So what seems like racial progress is actually more of the same old system of hegemonic white beauty. This trend is an example of the flexibility of capitalism, sexism, and racism. At a point when the ideology of beauty came under fire for not reflecting the beauty of women of color, and there was a possibility of insurgence, the power structure shifted its strategy to include women of color in such a way as to never disrupt the reigning beauty of white aesthetics and culture. No one knows what a feminist insurgency against the beauty regime would look like, but it might include a more public and lively discussion of beauty rituals and a possible rejection of many coercive beauty rituals. In order to avoid this and to maintain the multi-billion dollar industries that thrive on the pursuit of white beauty, the image-makers and publicists for these companies included a selected number of women of color in their advertisements, but none of those women had bodies or faces that challenged the dominant notion of white beauty. In fact, many have argued that the growing number of light-skinned, Anglo featured women of color in beauty ads encourages women of color consumers to purchase treatments and procedures to Anglicize their bodies, thus emulating brown and black versions of white beauty.

Although few people would disagree that women of color are purchasing high numbers of procedures that intentionally or unintentionally Anglicize their facial features, it is the meaning of this trend upon which many scholars and cosmetic surgery industry professionals disagree. Many have responded to the charge that women of color are regularly engaging in "whitening" beauty activities by relativizing the whole process. They argue that African American and Latina women may be choosing to change their noses to become narrower (an Anglo look), but white women are purchasing collagen injections to make their lips bigger (a typically African American trait). People of color may wish to be lighter, but white women are always in the tanning booth trying to get darker. This line of reasoning attempts to de-racinate the ideology of beauty by simply saying that the grass is always greener on the other side. This rhetorical strategy is another example of the colorblind discourse on contemporary race relations. It provides a way of deflecting racial domination and evading discussions of white privilege. White women who want to tan and make their lips bigger are not engaging in the same racial change practices that women of color are at all. White women are free to dabble in cosmetic procedures without ever losing their racial status as white. A tan white woman is still a white woman. A light-skinned or Anglo featured woman of color, however, can expect different treatment, and a greater share of resources, because she seems closer to white, or may be perceived as mixed-race. In fact, not only are white women not transgressing racial boundaries by purchasing bigger lips, they are actually reinforcing existing racial stereotypes about African American and Latino/a sexuality. White women purchase collagen injections for fuller lips because it is sexy. That sexiness is directly related to the stereotypic oversexualization of African Americans and Latino/as by way of big lips, wide hips, and larger buttocks. So cosmetic procedures chosen by women of color elevate whiteness in status, and some cosmetic procedures chosen by white women also elevate whiteness in status by degrading and oversexualizing blackness and brownness.

It is important to keep in mind that people make rational decisions to Anglicize their features in order to maximize their economic gain, through jobs, education, or even potential mates. On an individual basis, many women and men of color may decide to have nose surgery or other cosmetic procedures to make their features less African or Indian or Asian, and more European, or Western, though these decisions are rarely articulated in this racial manner. Their decisions are rational in a micro-level analysis. Individuals are likely to earn more money or move up higher in their occupations because of their more Anglo features. However, on a macro-level, these decisions are not rational at all.[40] As individuals continue to change their faces to be more European and to get higher rewards for simulating whiteness, the unaltered brown and black masses continue to pay a penalty for their more Indian or African features. In the long run, the practice of Anglicizing features through cosmetic surgery just perpetuates the inequality the individual is trying to escape. In this case, the master's tools will never dismantle the master's house. As Audre Lorde argued, oppressed people cannot use the tools of the master, in this case cosmetic surgery, to achieve Anglo physical features to topple the master's house of racism.[41] Individually, cosmetic surgery does allow for some escape of racial penalties associated with discrimination, but in the long run, cosmetic surgery just enables a system crippled from racism and dysfunction to remain alive a little longer. If worth and humanity continue to be based on Anglo conformity, then the larger social structures of racism that denigrate black and brown culture and aesthetics will never be dismantled.

# 5

## THE BEAUTY QUEUE
### *Advantages of Light Skin*

We always laughed in my dorm that the first month of school really light-skinned girls got dates. Then the brown-skinned girls
started getting dates. And finally by Christmas when all these
relationships were breaking up maybe the darker-skinned girls
would get a date.[1]

Pearl Marsh, a darker-skinned woman, told this story to sociologist
Maxine Leeds Craig for her study on black women and the politics of
beauty. Marsh's description of black women rank ordered by skin color is
not an anomaly. The high status of light-skinned women in the dating and
marriage market is an endemic feature in both the African American and
Mexican American communities. Marsh describes what I call a "beauty
queue." The beauty queue is a rank ordering of women from lightest
to darkest where the lightest get the most perks and rewards, dates for
example, and the darkest women get the least. This chapter outlines the
enormous and oppressive role of beauty in women's lives and explores
the advantages that light skin brings its wearers.

"Because beauty is asymmetrically assigned to the feminine role,
women are defined as much by their looks as by their deeds," writes Rita
Freedman, author of *Beauty Bound*.[2] In other words, in a sexist society
women's bodies indicate their worth, more often than their minds or
actions. Because "beauty" is a cultural construction, it is informed by
other kinds of societal status characteristics, most significantly race.

69

This helps explain why in the United States, where white racism still operates, light skin is often associated with beauty. Beauty also acts as a status characteristic that affects women's ability to get jobs or choose a spouse.[3] With these ideas in mind, this chapter explores how cultural assumptions about beauty and skin color affect the lives of Mexican American and African American women in their own voices.

This is the first qualitative and comparative examination of the attitudes of African American and Mexican American women regarding skin tone issues in everyday life.[4] Conversations with the women interviewees suggest that skin color stratification has both similar and different meanings in the African American and Mexican American communities.[5] The women I spoke with revealed an intense concern about light skin color as a status characteristic. Light skin was seen as a device for approval in families, as well as a near pre-requisite for the designation "beautiful." It was also a focal point of jealousies between female friends and family members. Despite the claim by women of both groups that light skin was considered more beautiful by society than dark, significant differences remain in just how these skin color politics played out in each community.

Notions of beauty are so closely related to color that the terms "light-skinned" and "pretty" were nearly synonymous. This conflation of concepts was particularly true among Mexican American women because in Spanish *güera* means both "light" and "pretty." The English equivalent would be "fair" which also means "light" or "white-skinned" and "pretty." The famous quote from the story *Snow White* serves as a great reminder of this double meaning, when the evil stepmother asks the mirror, "Who is the fairest of them all?" The mirror replies, "Snow White." She is after all, young and beautiful, and as her name implies, undoubtedly white.

Skin color affects women's lives in such important ways because women are so often evaluated by their physical attractiveness. Because physical appearance is such a crucial aspect of female value, (it is arguably more important than character or competence) the more beauty one possesses, the better off she will be when competing for resources such as jobs, education, or even spouses in the marriage market. In fact, the statistical analysis of the importance of skin color in chapter 3 revealed strong advantages for African American and Mexican American women in some or all of these areas.

In order to further theorize how beauty operates to rank order women, I use the concept of the beauty queue. The beauty queue explains how sexism and racism interact to create a queue of women from the lightest to the darkest, where the lightest get the most resources and the darkest get the least. The lightest women get access to more resources because not only are they lighter-skinned and therefore racially privileged, but their light skin is interpreted in our culture as more beautiful and therefore they also are privileged as beautiful women. The conflation of beauty and light skin is part of how racial aesthetics operate—lighter-skinned people with more Anglicized features are viewed by most in American culture (either consciously or unconsciously) as superior.

I use the metaphor of a queue in this discussion of beauty and color for three reasons. First, the concept of a queue shows that women are rank ordered by men and by one another, according to their beauty quotient (totality of physical traits) and consequently, according to their skin color. Second, the concept shows how all women are evaluated by their physical appearances to the point that beauty has become a form of social capital for women. Beauty works as capital in the sense that the more of it one has, the more able one will be to marry a high-status husband, and the more able one will be to increase her own income and education. Third, I use the metaphor of the queue because it invokes the image of women waiting in line for male partners. Much of the interaction among women over skin color and beauty is centered on the perceived competition for male partners. In the following analysis I show how beauty works as an ideology and how the beauty queue, and each person's place in it, is implicitly understood by all women.

A significant number of interviewees admitted at some time in their lives wanting to have lighter skin, lighter eyes, or longer hair. Both African American and Mexican American interviewees believed that light-skinned women were attractive and many African American, but fewer Mexican American women found light-skinned men of their groups to be attractive. Skin color, eye color, and hairstyles that most approximated whites were highly revered and often sought after through colored contacts, hair straightening, and hair coloring by women of both ethnic groups. However, intertwined with the high value on a white bodily aesthetic, was a simultaneous distrust and resentment of women who did possess these white-like traits. This was particularly true for African American women. Mexican American women were more likely to report feeling jealous or resentful of lighter-skinned family members, especially sisters or female cousins. I begin my discussion with the African American interviews, then I will discuss the Mexican American women's interviews, and I end this chapter with a comparison of their experiences and a discussion of forms of reflection and resistance.

## AFRICAN AMERICAN WOMEN AND COLOR

Among the African American participants, the most frequent and consistent characterization was that of the "light-skinned, stuck-up, snobby, pretty, black girl." This stereotype came up in almost every interview with an African American, whether dark or light-skinned. Many dark-skinned women discussed this characterization as a truth, or as previously believing in its reality when they were young; and most light-skinned black women discussed battling regularly with this. In general, both lighter-skinned and darker-skinned women agreed that as a rule, light-skinned women were considered by men to be more attractive than dark-skinned women. This belief left many darker-skinned women feeling hostile and resentful toward the lighter women. Belinda, who is a dark-skinned African American woman said,

> In terms of female-female relationships, I think color affects how we treat each other. Like if you're lighter and I think you're better, and I think the guys want you, then I won't treat you nicely. I'll take every opportunity to ignore you, or not tell you something, or keep you out of my little group of friends, because really I feel threatened, so I want to punish you because you have it better than me.

Belinda is strikingly honest in revealing that she feels threatened by lighter-skinned women and their attractiveness to black men. She also admits that sometimes she feels lighter women are "better" than she is. Her way of coping with the unfair value placed on light skin is to outcast lighter women from her own circle of friends. Belinda clearly sees her hostile actions toward lighter women as "punishment" for having privileges that she does not. Her experience is not unique. Lighter-skinned women often reported feeling socially ostracized and resented by darker-skinned African American women. Belinda's hostile feelings are a compelling example of the pain that can be caused by the emphasis on skin color in the African American community.

I asked Kitara, another dark-skinned black woman I interviewed, to describe how color affected her as a young girl.

> Both my parents are dark-skinned black, too, and they wanted me to have the whole black pride thing.... We never considered skin bleaching or anything like that. We just dealt with it...It hurts when you're younger because you are the butt of jokes. For the longest time you feel like you are just so ugly. I was dark-skinned,

tall, and skinny, and that was a bad combination. I was really quiet.
I would relax around my friends, but I was quiet.

Kitara's story is particularly compelling because it shows that even
well meaning parents, who want you to "have the whole black pride
thing" cannot protect their children from the strong cultural messages
that denigrate black skin. Kitara implies that she experienced frequent
anxiety over the teasing she encountered when she says, "I would relax
around my friends." One can imagine a child who is often embattled
with other kids over skin color, and can only let her guard down among
friends and family.

Throughout the interviews with African American women, the theme
of competition for male partners was constant. The demographic reality
of the African American community today exacerbates the perception
(and reality) of competition for scarce male partners because of the un-
balanced sex ratio of African Americans. Because of the large numbers
of African American men currently incarcerated, underemployed, and
unemployed, many African American women feel a market scarcity of
"marriageable" men.[6] This scarcity leads to increased tension and competition among African American women for the limited number of
potential male partners, thus increasing animosity over issues of beauty
and skin color.

Another interviewee, Pamela, who is dark-skinned, talked about how
her hostility toward lighter-skinned women grew into hatred and limited
her relationships with other black women.

> Color has always come up in my life. Always. It's bad to be dark.
> It's good to be light—when I was growing up. I will say that I
> started to resent lighter women. I have a friend of mine now,
> she's [light-skinned]. When I lived next door to her I hated her.
> She's beautiful. And I thought, "God, I hate you." I never talked
> to her because she was beautiful. But, color has always come up.
> It's like how in slavery times the darker person would be out in
> the fields and the lighter person would be up in the house. That's
> still going on because the lighter is closer to white and since it's
> closer to white it's better.

As discussed earlier, light skin and beauty were frequently used interchangeably by the women I spoke with. Pamela now regrets her feelings
of hatred toward her neighbor who is now very close to her. This is not to
say that her feelings of distrust were unwarranted, but they limited her
willingness to explore friendships with other black women. As Patricia

Hill Collins writes, "Sometimes the pain most deeply felt is the pain that Black women inflict on one another."[7] This comment captures the extreme emotions that were evident in the interviews I conducted. Many African American women were extremely upset by the level of hostility and resentment they witnessed, or were responsible for, on both sides of the color line.

Karla, a light-skinned black woman, told me about her anxieties about skin color issues before she went to college.

> Before I came to [this university] I had this nightmare that I had two black roommates and I just walked in and they were like "Yaarrrgh!" [*said in a hostile voice*]. It was horrible. I mean I have nightmares about this stuff. I don't feel like I'm racist, it just makes me feel really sad. There is one black girl on my floor in the dorms and we're kind of buddying up and it makes me feel really good.

Karla's story is emblematic of the longing for female friendship and connection that is so often stymied by tension from skin color differences. Light-skinned Karla had so much fear of rejection from dark-skinned women that she had nightmares about it. But beneath those anxieties was a real yearning to connect with other black women that she says "makes me feel really good."

This tension among African American women was not only felt by darker-skinned women, but also by lighter-skinned women. Aisha is a mixed-race (black and white) woman, and identified as African American. She expressed regret and frustration as she described a history of conflict between herself and darker-skinned black women.

> I can only say that I've had problems growing up, as far as my race, with full black females and for the simple fact that... I'm sure everyone that has talked to you has said this, but, they just look at you and say, "Oh, you just think you are so cute just because you're mixed and you got good hair." I remember when I was in high school it was my freshman year. There was this guy, he was black, but you know he just didn't interest me. He asked me for my number and I was like, "No, that's okay." I just wasn't interested. Well, these girls must have been friends of his or something, and two or three of them got pissed off because I didn't want to talk to him and they said, "Oh, you just think you're too good and you can't talk to him because you just think you're too cute." And that pissed me off. Even to this day I am still uncomfortable to walk

into a room with a bunch of full black girls because I feel like they just look at me up and down and think, "Oh, you just think that you are so cute." I have always thought that it was envy in a way, not because I am the better of anyone, not at all, but I think even they feel that lighter is better. Maybe because they've been told for so long that dark is not pretty and dark is bad.

Aisha, like many of the other women I interviewed, invoked the image of the light-skinned girl who thinks she is "too cute," although she does so in order to challenge it. Aisha makes a compelling observation when she says that she thinks even the darker-skinned girls think lighter is better. She touches on the serious damage internalized racism can do to individuals, as well as to communities. Interestingly, Aisha describes her struggles with other black girls as not only about color, but also racial identity. Despite the fact that she identifies as African American, even though she is mixed, she describes the struggle over color not with "darker-skinned girls," but with "full black girls." For Aisha, and other mixed-race African American women I interviewed, skin color was closely tied to racial identity and resentment toward lighter-skinned girls was synonymous with resentment toward mixed-race girls. Aisha describes being harassed by darker-skinned/"full black" girls in high school and characterized herself as a "victim" of their teasing. Several of the light-skinned African American women reported being "victimized" in various ways by darker-skinned African American women. This included being socially sanctioned, being harassed, ostracized, and in one extreme case even included threats of violence. Their alleged "victimization" is a surprising inversion of the larger system of colorism that victimizes darker-skinned people in many ways. This is an important point discursively as well. Clearly, darker-skinned women are at a disadvantage in terms of social status. Yet, it is lighter-skinned women who consistently, throughout each interview, characterized themselves as victims of dark-skinned women.

One of the notable exceptions to that trend is Simone. She is a light-skinned, mixed-race, African American woman who lived in Europe in the 1980s. I asked her to describe her relationships with other black women here in the United States.

My experience has been that black women in general do not like me. That has been my experience. Except for the ones that I've already come to know really well. I've had women follow me around the supermarket, just mad. I don't really know what that's about.... They're not my enemy. I'm sorry that's going on.... The women and I, we just don't seem to get along. I understand. I really do and I don't want to be their enemy. I don't want to be their target, but I don't hold that against them. I have an intuitive idea of how they feel about me or how they see me and I've been there. That's very similar to how I felt about these blonde, blue-eyed women with their blue mascara in the 80s. They irked me. They bothered me because I just felt they were inherently in a better position all the way around than I was.... They had that privilege and they used it. They never took responsibility for that privilege and they never acknowledged that I didn't have that privilege. I think that that's part of what's going on between light-skinned women and dark-skinned women.

Interestingly, it is Simone's own experience on the lower end of the beauty queue in relation to white women that provides her with some insight into the psychology and emotions around skin color for African American women. Her frequent use of the word "enemy" captures the hostility often present in relations between lighter and darker black women. Simone, like many of the light-skinned black women I spoke with, said she knew where the anger and resentment of dark-skinned women was coming from. She understood their anger and found it justified.

Delilah is a black woman with a medium brown complexion and very long, curly black hair. Though she does have friendships with other African American women, she reports much tension over "the hair issue" and recounts the following story about the first elementary school she attended.

The school in that area was majority Filipino and African American, no white people. I went there for a month and then my mother took me out of that school because ... girls tried to cut my hair off, they said black girls aren't supposed to have long hair. Black girls hated me. Girls would say, "Oh, you stole my boyfriend." And I said, "I don't even know your boyfriend." They kept saying things like, "I'm gonna beat your ass with a baseball bat ... " They chased me down. The school couldn't do anything about it until one of the girls did something to me. And my mom said, "I'm not going to wait for one of these girls to kill her," so I transferred and I went to a school about 30 minutes away.

Delilah's experience is an extreme example of jealousy and distrust among African American girls. Long hair is highly sought after in the black community and is typically associated with whites. The booming hair care industry that includes wigs, weaves, and braids is evidence of the pursuit of long hair.[8] It is rare to find a young black girl who is not "trying to grow her hair out." In fact, many girls and women wear their hair in braids or use hair extensions, not for the Afrocentric look it creates, but sometimes for the opposite reason, to allow their hair to grow out while it is braided. Belinda told me about recently putting her hair in braids.

> Yeah, I got braids to give my hair a break from the chemicals and let it get healthier, so it could grow. But then, that's the whole thing about growing your hair long. Everybody's talking about growing their hair. Everybody wants long pretty hair.

Long hair, often called "good hair" is an important corollary to light skin for high status and beauty in the African American community.[9] In fact, the "good hair/bad hair" issue is so prevalent in the black community, several authors have written children's books to try to destigmatize kinky or nappy hair.[10]

In her reflective essay about race and feminism, activist and writer Michele Wallace describes a childhood game she and her sister would play involving the tying of scarves around their short braids to mimic long, flowing hair. She writes, "There was a time when I would have called that wanting to be white, yet the real point of the game was being feminine. Being feminine *meant* being white to us."[11] Wallace touches on a crucial point in trying to understand whiteness and womanhood. True femininity is still defined in relation to whiteness. The personality and physical traits most associated with white women: helplessness, dependence, light skin, and blonde hair are those most closely aligned with femininity. Feminine girls or women are white, or at least look white. Pretty girls are white, or at least look white. This demonstrates the shared meanings of whiteness, femininity, and beauty. Although Wallace came of age a generation before most of the women I interviewed, messages about femininity, light skin, and long hair seem to have changed little. The participants in this study expressed having learned similar lessons from both adults and other young people in their communities.

Although many of the interviewees had painful experiences around color that were still fresh in their minds, a few were able to step back from their experiences and evaluate them. I asked Regina, who is a light-skinned African American woman, to describe the issue of skin color among black women.

Well...I hate it! I really hate it! It bothers me. It's made me so bitter towards women and I have a really big guard up all the time and I'm not really the first one to say, "Hi." I always thought someone had a problem with me, just by the way they looked, if they didn't smile or something. I completely attributed it to me being either mixed or light-skinned. I think they go hand in hand and I think it's terrible.

Regina expresses her anger and frustration at herself, as well as at the larger situation among black women. She describes how her own experiences have made her "bitter towards women" and less able to create relationships with other black women. She says she has a near paranoia about feeling hostility from other women that has resulted in her own self-defensiveness. Her self-described behavior of not saying "Hi" feeds the stereotype of light-skinned women as aloof and acting superior to others. Despite that, Regina was very concerned about the havoc that color politics had wreaked on her relationships with other African American women. It is also interesting to note that Regina also associates the tension and hostility between herself and other black women with her racial identity as a "mixed" person. In fact, she mentions being both light-skinned and mixed as potential reasons for her ongoing tensions with other black women. I will discuss the relationship between skin color and identity in more detail in the next chapter.

Aisha believed that color was such a significant issue in the African American community because it was a vehicle through which women competed for male partners. She was one of the few respondents who characterized the quest for beauty and status among women as a diversion from larger and more problematic gender relations between women and men in the African American community.

I think among black women more than any other group of women there is the most competition. I think they are so much in competition with each other that girls who are friends really don't trust their own friends. They still talk shit about their own friends. That's what I've never liked because I'm not that way. I think it's a terrible way to be. If we are going to be in conflict about anything it should be the men and the differences we have with them and how they try to oppress us from a gender perspective. I think it's so ugly really, and that's one of the best words I could use. It's just plain ugly to be in so much competition over men.

Aisha describes the "ugliness" of competition for men as harmful to black women's friendships, and a distraction from problems between men and women. Aisha and Regina both shared with me their concern about the situation among black women, but Aisha's thinking on the topic went even further because she suggests that distrust over color leaves other important community problems unaddressed. In fact, Aisha lays the foundation for the argument that I am trying to build, that competition among women over skin color is a diversion from larger oppressive systems such as racism and sexism. She describes the internalized racism among many African Americans that results in the lack of trust or intimacy in some African American women's relationships.

## MEXICAN AMERICAN WOMEN AND COLOR

Attitudes toward skin color and beauty were similar in many ways between African American and Mexican American women. Participants from both groups thought that, as a rule, in order to be considered pretty one had to have light skin. Mexican Americans, as well as African Americans shared painful experiences of being the "dark" one in the family, or of feeling less favored than lighter-skinned family members. Of course, dark skin means different things in each community. Among the African Americans I spoke with, dark skin was not necessarily an important class distinction. Skin color was more of a racial marker; revealing a mixed-race background through light skin, for instance, earned high community status. However, in the Mexican American community, being dark-skinned was linked to being Indian and that contained a whole host of meanings about color, class, modernization, and intelligence. The dark-skinned Mexican American participants described trying to avoid being seen as *India*, and Mexican American participants of all colors reported being familiar with negative stereotypes about Indians in Mexico.

Although the trend to assign negative racial meanings to darker-skinned people is similar, the Mexican American interviewees did not report the high levels of distrust and animosity among Mexican American women that black women reported in their community. The Mexican American interviewees frequently referred to the term *la güera* which is similar in meaning to "fair" in English; both mean "light" and "pretty" simultaneously. Some of the interviewees considered themselves to be *las güeras*, and others grew up as *las prietas*, "the dark ones."

Barbara is a light-skinned Mexican American woman. I asked her to describe what "looking Indian" meant.

To look Indian means to look dark, to have slanted eyes, high cheekbones. Especially dark, especially dark. That's what gets pointed out. That's how I always grew up with it. They're always the ones with the nicknames. My brother was the really dark one in my family and he was called the *prieto* which means the dark one. I think it's paternalistic. I think it has negative historical roots, but I think it changes to make it affectionate. You know, "*un negrita*" and stuff like that. In Mexico it's *mi morena*, but I think that that's the way darker-skinned Chicanos are looked upon, to be more Indian. Which is the way that Mexico looks at Indians, to be not as modern, not as sophisticated. It's just not as pretty, or not as . . . white. Not as attractive.

Barbara points out an ongoing tension in Mexican American culture: the negative and yet affectionate terms such as "*mi negrita*," "*mi prieto*" and "*mi morena*." She describes them as paternalistic because they make people appear child-like by often using "*mi*" meaning "my." This may imply ownership, superiority, or affection. These terms are reminiscent of negative and paternalistic terms that African Americans were called during slavery like "little darkies" or "pickaninnies." Barbara, like Regina and Aisha, has reflected on this topic enough to have ambivalence about what previously seemed liked harmless nicknames. It is also important to note the strong racial language Barbara invoked about looking Indian. The discourses of modernity and civilization are still present when describing Mexican Indians and are therefore still symbolized when evaluating dark skin color, because it is associated with Indians.

Even young children learn early lessons about skin color and status. Alicia works at an elementary school and describes a conversation between two children there.

I work as a TA at an elementary school and this little girl started saying, "Teacher! Teacher!" She was really mad and she said, "Jose called me an *India*!" And I looked at her and thought, why does she think that is so bad? She was really upset about it like he called her a bad name. And these were two Latino children. And being called "*India*," that really struck her like, "That was so evil why did you call me that?" I noticed that.

Even Alicia was surprised by the young children's sharp adherence to racial hierarchies. Both children in the interaction knew that to be considered *India* was degrading. And the girl's appeal to Alicia as an authority figure shows that the girl expected Alicia to also appreciate the gravity of the epithet. Some might want to chalk this incident up to child's play. And though teasing is a part of all children's experience, racial epithets are not and many adults who received those insults as children still harbor the wounds. This teasing does not end in elementary school. I asked Isabel, a dark-skinned Mexican American woman, if skin color ever came up in her high school experience.

> Yeah, I had a friend who looked white, but she spoke Spanish because she was Mexican. She was very popular because she was so light....A lot of the darker girls were not [popular]. It was a good thing to be light. And a lot of the kids would make fun of me because I would get dark. So they would call me "nigger. " And I would take it like, "Yeah, so?" I could care less. What was I going to do? I couldn't do anything about that.

Isabel reveals many meanings of skin color in her comments, most notably the tension between Blacks and Chicanos in Los Angeles as exemplified in calling dark-skinned Mexican Americans "niggers." Although for most Mexican Americans, dark skin is closely associated with indigenous identity, for others, it is also associated with blackness. For Mexican Americans and other people of color who internalize white racist norms, blackness is something to avoid just as much as Indianness.

Several Mexican American women I spoke with described competitions and jealousies with female family members over skin color differences. Catalina describes the preferential treatment her cousin received in the family because of her light skin color.

> My cousin's hair came out really light so she looks Anglo. Except for her features, her facial features. But her skin color, eyes, and hair look Anglo. Even when we were little, I remember they used to say to her, "*Hola güera!*" I think they used to think of her as prettier than all my other cousins because she was lighter. I tended to stick to my other cousin more, maybe because we were more closer in skin color. I think in a way when we were younger, we were jealous of her, just because a lot of people paid attention to her and said, "Oh, she's so cute! Look at those beautiful green eyes."

Here Catalina reinforces the idea that in Mexican American culture, lighter skin is considered to be more beautiful. Although the term *güera* is a compliment, it is a racially charged one. Catalina describes feeling inferior to her light-skinned cousin who was always being complimented on her light skin, light eyes, and thus her beauty. Catalina's story about being compared to other female relatives was common throughout the interviews with Mexican American women and reminiscent of the jealousy described among African American women, although those were not typically family relationships.

Alicia, a darker-skinned Mexican American woman, told me about her own experiences with the quest for physical beauty and how her friends and family encouraged her to look lighter, or at least to avoid looking any darker. It was clear to her that having darker skin was to be avoided through use of makeup, clothes, or hair coloring. It was not overtly associated with attractiveness to men, but was definitely a status issue.

> I'll dye my hair and my mom will say, "Don't dye it that color it makes you look darker." More value is placed on being light. The girls they make comments like, "Oh, did you see her? She's so pretty. Her eyes, they're so light." The hair color is brought up a lot. "Oh, try this color, it will make you look lighter." Even with lighter skin, my friend dyed her hair jet black and everybody was like, "Yeah, that looks good, it makes you look lighter. I like that."

Alicia expressed her feelings about this topic with exasperation. She seemed to feel that people were overly concerned with color and that there was no such thing as being too light, as evidenced by the fact that even light-skinned people were trying to look lighter. Alicia told this story with some feelings of shame about her appearance, but she clearly had moved in her thinking over the years. She told the story in the past tense and described it as outrageous and unfair, showing that although she experienced colorism, she did not buy into it.

Patricia Zavella's research supports Alicia's contention of color consciousness in the Mexican American community. Zavella writes, "Although some change is occurring regarding the preferred body image, our society still values women who are white—and blond in particular—and who have European features."[12] Zavella goes on to argue that, "Individuals within Chicano communities may reflect this devaluation, or even internalize it, so that physical features are often noted and evaluated: Skin color in particular is commented on, with las güeras (light-skinned ones) being appreciated and las prietas (dark-skinned ones) being admonished and devalued."[13] The value of light skin is so enmeshed in Mexican American cultural values that many people do not even realize the pain they cause others by making evaluative comments about skin color.

Alicia was very similar to other women in the study in her reaction to color issues: She was frustrated and hurt by the devaluation of dark skin, but she did not have a sense of why color was so important in our society or how this hierarchy was started. This disjuncture between colorism and beauty standards demonstrates that most women do not have a rubric for understanding skin color politics that includes racism. Issues of beauty and color were often described by people as silly, or petty, but not usually as a part of a larger system of racism. Beauty has become such a powerful economic force in this country that it is seen as independent of other forces of oppression, such as racism and sexism. Making the connection between these concepts is crucial in order to expose the subtle ways that racism and sexism persist in the lives of women of color.

Another Mexican American interviewee, Elena, said that she believed that values of color were so ingrained in Mexican American consciousness, they were often hard to detect. She describes how colorism is almost an unconscious process.

> I don't think that people mean to say that lighter people are pretty, but I know that in general when someone comments on someone being really pretty, it's generally a light person. But I notice when someone's talking about a girl who's pretty, or even a guy who's good looking, they're usually light.

Elena describes how attractiveness is typically noticed only in people who are light-skinned. In this way, she says, people are not overtly saying that only light-skinned women are attractive, but the message is still the same. The cumulative effect of naming beauty only in light-skinned people still communicates that dark skin is undesirable. The corollary to this phenomenon is qualifying beauty in dark-skinned women. For instance, the saying, "She's dark, but she's pretty" is a common one in both the Mexican American and African American communities. It shows that darkness is not normally associated with beauty, but in this exceptional case, the woman in question is dark, *but* pretty—she is able to transcend her skin color. The exception proves the rule.

Linda, a light-skinned Mexican American, confirms Elena's statements about lightness and beauty when she describes the special treatment that her sister received as a result of her Anglo-like characteristics.

> My sister is lighter-skinned than I am and her hair is like a lighter brown than mine and her eyes are hazel, like greenish. And they call her *güera*. I don't know if you've heard that term before. And they're just like "Oh, her eyes" and "She's so beautiful." When it comes to color, like skin color, the lighter the better.

Linda states it plainly, "the lighter the better." Her experiences are particularly interesting because although she is light-skinned herself, she felt that in comparison to her sister she was not as light, and therefore not the one identified as *la güera*. This inherent comparison is further evidence of the beauty queue. Women are rank ordered. So even some light-skinned women lose out on the status of their skin color if they are being directly compared to people who are even lighter than they are. Her sentiments echo those of other women who were onlookers to the affections and compliments of lighter-skinned female relatives. Most of the women I interviewed compared themselves, and felt compared by others, to other women in their families: sisters, cousins, mothers, and aunts. The elements of comparison, judging, and evaluation were found throughout my interviews with Mexican American women. Interestingly, most of the women, regardless of color, felt that they were on the losing end of those comparisons, ultimately feeling inadequate, less light-skinned, and therefore less pretty than other female family members. It is also important to note that the Mexican American participants largely reported being compared to other female relatives, not males. Although skin color is still a status predictor for both men and women the strong connection of skin color to beauty and the privileges that this connection accrues seems to apply most consistently to women.

Many Mexican American respondents described their families in terms of who was lightest and who was darkest and how their skin tones affected their experiences both inside and outside of the family. These descriptions often included family nicknames regarding color or more simply *la güera* and *el prieto*. This practice points to the importance of skin color as an identifier in many Mexican American families.

> The one person we do tease in the family about color is my uncle Art. He is very light. His whole family is light with blonde hair and light eyes. So it's always kind of a joke. And he developed a country accent because he used to hang out with a lot of white kids in Florida. They would say to him, "Oh, you're the light sheep of the family!" I guess my grandma, when he was born, she thought they switched babies on her because he was so light. She cried about it and everything.

> They used to call my aunt, who is dark, "la negra." But they call me "the white one." That's me. I don't know if that's a positive thing or a negative thing.

Yeah, they used to call me "morena" or "prieta" because I was the darkest one of the family. And my other sister, they used to call her "guera" which means light one.

All of these examples from the interviews with Mexican Americans show the important role that skin color plays in family dynamics. In some families, skin color related nicknames were used in playful, more benign ways, and in others they were painful barbs that reinforced status differences among the members. Skin color related nicknames were commonly reported among almost all of the Mexican American women I spoke with and most women agreed that after the gender, skin color was one of the first traits of newborn babies commented upon in their families.

## SKIN COLOR, MEDIA, AND SEXUALITY

Light-skinned women of color continue to be reflected back to us through the media as the most desirable or most attractive black and Latina women.[14] In fact, a cursory glance at today's media images reveals that many of the women who represent African Americans on the small and big screens are mixed-race black women. This is significant because they are much more likely to be extremely light-skinned, have straight or less kinky hair and possess European features. Mega-celebrities Halle Berry, Alicia Keyes, and Vanessa Williams are all examples of this phenomenon. The same is true for the Latinas that have risen to celebrity status. Light-skinned Latina women of various nationalities are presented in media outlets as the most beautiful. Jennifer Lopez, who is Puerto Rican, and Salma Hayek, who is Mexican American, are both examples of light-skinned Latina icons. Additional examples of this trend of representation are found in the extremely popular Spanish telenovelas. In the novelas, affluent women are almost always white in their physical appearance (light skin, blonde hair, and light eyes), while poor women or daughters of maids are darker-skinned. This shows the close correlation between color and class in Latin America and in Latino culture. Even though most of this book is focusing on the Mexican American experience and not a broader Latino experience, the consumption of Latino images tends to be pan-ethnic phenomenon. Although Mexican Americans dominate the U.S. Latino media market, celebrities of many nations are represented—but they are consistently white or light. It is also interesting to note that Spaniards like Antonio Banderas and Penelope Cruz are also marketed as Latino celebrities even though they are European and obviously white or light-skinned.

An examination of these media images begs the question, how do women of color respond to the constant media messages that light is right? Many of the women I interviewed reported confusion and frustration as they dealt with the many media images that devalued their own beauty. In my interview with Marsha, a dark-skinned African American woman, she discussed her own moments of reflection about her body type and contemporary notions of beauty. She also describes a common struggle: The difficulty of distinguishing her own tastes from those that the media has created.

> I work in the market and right next to where I work are all the girly magazines like *Glamour* and *Vogue*. And every month it's white females. And that's supposed to be pretty. And they have this ideal white female who is supposed to be skinny. And what I'm realizing is, I'm black. I'm going to have big hips; I'm gonna have thighs, a butt. So maybe, the guys don't like that because they see that as being fat, instead of being part of who they are…. There's this new model, she's kind of dark-skinned. She's really dark-skinned and she really doesn't have any hair. She has the full lips and stuff so she's really ethnic looking. To me she's not attractive, but I'm trying to figure out is that because she's dark-skinned and she doesn't have the long hair? And she has the full lips. Am I falling into society's trap? Or is she just not pretty?

Marsha describes how the print media influences both women and men into accepting certain physical traits, namely European or white traits, as more beautiful than others. Marsha is coming to terms with the permanence of her own identity as a black woman and how her own body type and its beauty are very different from that of the white women featured on the cover of popular beauty magazines. Marsha describes struggling with her feelings about a dark-skinned, African-looking model, unable to sort out her own opinions from those that the media have prescribed. Her dilemma was echoed throughout several of the interviews. Jocelyn describes the difficulty of understanding how one comes to her own opinion about beauty, without the influence of the white-dominated media.

> I try not to be influenced by the magazines. I'm the one who also says, "This is because of me, not just because of what I see." But

I think it is subliminal, too, why I want to lose weight. Yeah, I want to be thinner, but it's also because I know what the image of beauty is to a lot of people. That's why I keep trying to achieve that.... All of my roommates are on Weight Watchers right now. And in the black community they're all like, "Yeah, we like big butts," but then they want a thin girl. It's weird.

Both Jocelyn and Marsha's stories demonstrate how our tastes and preferences are socially constructed, and rarely our own.

The trend of an almost exclusive focus on images of light-skinned women does not seem to hold true for African American or Mexican American men in the media. Increasingly, darker-skinned men are featured in media campaigns as highly sexualized and attractive. In ad campaigns, movies, and other media outlets it has become common to see images of darker-skinned Latino and black men. Although on the surface, this may look like racial progress, this trend actually coincides with long-held beliefs of African American and Mexican American men as hyper-sexualized and sexually dangerous.[15] Both groups of men have been characterized throughout history as hypersexual (the black Mandingo and the Latin lover) and as rapists who threaten the chastity of white women and white nationhood.[16] So, even though there are more images of dark-skinned men of color in the media as sexy and attractive, the underlying racial meanings of black and brown bodies as sexual playgrounds or as sexually deviant remains unchanged.

There are alternative ways of making sense of the highly sexual dark-skinned black or Latino male image, however. Several interviewees defined darker-skinned men as more attractive than lighter-skinned men. Barbara, one of the Mexican American participants, talked about her preference for dating darker-skinned men. She attached this preference to Mexican pride, but also to a desire to value what the larger society does not.

Usually, I prefer a darker-skinned man. It's attached to sexualness, virility, being more Latino. And I think it is in a way, ... you want to appreciate what isn't liked in a larger context.

On one hand, Barbara seems to buy into stereotypical images of dark-skinned men as more sexually potent than lighter skinned men. However, Barbara also demonstrates an understanding of light-skin privilege in mainstream or white society and she describes making an effort to work against that privilege by "appreciating what isn't liked in a larger context." Darker skin is more Latino to her, and therefore more sexy. Ethnic identity is closely tied to sexual desirability for Barbara and for several other participants. I will discuss this issue in more detail in the following chapter.

Not all participants described darker-skinned black and Latino men as more attractive than lighter-skinned men. In fact, a handful of women, including Rochelle described a pattern of liking or dating light-skinned men of color. In the following passage, Rochelle, an African American, describes how she is slowly coming to terms with the idea that she has chosen past boyfriends in part because of their light skin.

> There was a time when I would have argued so adamantly that I was not quote unquote colorstruck, but in my attempts to introspect on that I have come to realize and honestly acknowledge that maybe I do have an issue about color. Because when I look back, my friends have always said, "Oh Rochelle, you like those light guys. You like those guys with that hair." And a certain kind of guy. And I have never thought of myself as having a type, but when I look back at these boyfriends, what are the distinguishing characteristics? The majority tended to be of a fairer skin color, tended to have a finer texture of hair, tended to be multiracial for the most part. And I would often try to cover that up and say that I'm just interested in exotic people. And I still think that that may have something to do with it. But when it really boils down to it, I realize that I do tend to date guys that are about my skin color or maybe lighter. I don't think that was something that I really did consciously, but then at the same time I want to say there must be something driving that, but I've never really gotten at the heart of it.

Rochelle's comments are particularly insightful because she has already done some thinking about these issues in her own life. She seemed embarrassed to admit her bias for lighter-skinned men and she went as far as calling herself "colorstruck," an insult in the African American community. However, Rochelle's comments are an example of the still powerful preferences for light skin even in men. This is also evidenced through research that shows lighter-skinned black and Mexican American men receiving higher wages and more years of education than their darker-skinned counterparts.[17] It seems that light skin color is an asset to both men and women in many areas of life, but for women, light skin remains extremely important in the marriage market because of its close association with beauty in a way that is no longer as true for men.[18]

## INTERNALIZING RACISM AND SEXISM

The beauty queue is alive and well in the Mexican American and African American communities. Light-skinned women are privileged in many areas of life, including being defined as the most beautiful, by being at the front of the queue. However, there are also costs for those at the front of the queue—resentment and distrust from darker-skinned women, and possibly fewer opportunities for female friendship. The damage done to female friendships, by the presence of and adherence to the beauty queue, seems to be much more devastating in the African American community than in the Mexican American community. This may be due in part to competition over a perceived scarcity of men. Ironically, even when women are able to see the harm of the beauty queue and of color hierarchy, they often still adhere to it by wishing they were lighter, or had longer hair.

One of the most important themes in this chapter is the insidiousness of racism that manifests itself in colorism. Colorism is a systematic preference for lightness that stems from the larger and more potent system of racism. It is difficult to distinguish between our own innocent preferences for skin tones and the socially constructed hierarchy of skin tones informed by racism. Many have internalized this racism so deeply, that they can no longer recognize colorism and racism for what they are, and instead see them simply as individual tastes.

Frantz Fanon (1967) wrote about the quest for black people to lighten and whiten their race through intermarriage. On the topic of black men pursuing white women he takes on the voice of a black man who longs to be white. He writes, "I wish to be acknowledged not as black, but as white... By loving me she [a white woman] proves that I am worthy of white love. I am loved like a white man. I am a white man...I marry white culture, white beauty, white whiteness."[19] According to Fanon, the goal of whitening was motivated by a sense of self-hatred that was ingrained from centuries of French colonial rule. Not only had the land been colonized, but so too, had the minds, cultures, and value systems of the African people in Martinique and other French colonies. The black man in Fanon's quotation longs to be white because it is only through whiteness that his humanity can be acknowledged. This is the story of another segment of the African Diaspora, but it rings true for the experiences of colonized people of color here in the United States in many ways. At some point in their lives, many of the women I interviewed wanted lighter skin tones or more Anglo facial features. They were well aware of the privileges assigned to those who possess such traits. In fact, the white standards of beauty are so ingrained in our culture, that they seem removed from issues of race, completely separate. This makes the pursuit of beauty seem like a non-racial issue, when in fact it is acutely so.

This is an example of how hegemony works. The subjugated people rule themselves according to the laws of the powerful. Whites need no longer police the boundaries of race and status, because people of color have internalized their racial hierarchies. Kitara, a dark-skinned black woman, describes being teased about her dark complexion as a young girl.

> When I was a lot younger you have the jokes, the monkey jokes...I went to a black school and most of us were dark-skinned black, but it was still there. Nobody wanted to be all the way black. They tried to be, "You know I'm Indian" or something....It wasn't cool to be all the way black.

Kitara's painful story illustrates how African American people have internalized the racist beliefs of whites (monkey jokes) and inflicted them upon one another. According to Kitara, black children try to avoid the stigma of blackness by claiming some type of mixed race heritage ("You know I'm Indian"). In this case, whites need not even be present (an all black school) for racism and colorism to flourish. The hegemony of beauty and color works the same way. Many people of color have internalized racial hierarchies to such an extent that some women claw each other to get to the front of the beauty queue and conform to white standards of beauty. This is a tightly woven matrix of racism and sexism. Several of the women I interviewed commented on the ephemeral nature of colorism. They described it as everywhere, and yet hard to identify or point out.

> Even though I say I haven't seen it blatantly out there, it is still there. I don't know how, but subtly. It just seems like there is this thing where light-skinned girls are prettier and have nicer hair. I can't understand where it came from, but I feel like it's always there.

> I really don't see it as that big of a deal around the color issue, even though I know that it is a deal. I think it is a factor, but it's kind of like underground. No one really speaks about it very much, but it is there, kind of like racism to some extent. Like a lot of white people really don't want to talk about racism although it really exists, and they try to overlook it. Maybe it's to some extent like that.

Both of these quotations describe the way that colorism has seeped into everyday culture so that it is hard to clearly identify, even though everyone sees it. Many of the women I interviewed expressed similar seemingly contradictory sentiments. Color is not a significant issue because no one really talks about it, while at the same time saying that color remains an extremely divisive issue. This is part of the challenge of critically discussing colorism and racism.

Many people of color challenge one another to look more white and punish those who do not. Whites play their own role in this process, but African Americans and Mexican Americans play one as well.[20] Darker-skinned black women distrust or resent light-skinned women, and light-skinned black women often use the privileges they have to increase their social status above darker-skinned people. Mexican American women strive for lightness and feel rejected when compared to lighter female relatives, all the while desperately trying to avoid being grouped with the *Indios* and associated with backwardness. This is a method of the divide-and-conquer principle. While women of color are busy trying to be lighter and feeling resentful toward one another, men maintain their status as full subjects and white women and men maintain their racial privilege by having their own phenotype defined as most beautiful in relation to the African and Mexican/Indian aesthetics.

It is important to remember who benefits from the ideology of beauty and the beauty queue. Ultimately, both of these constructs serve to maintain sexism and racism because they objectify and commodify women and they value whiteness over brownness and blackness. The power of these systems has seeped into the cultures and consciousness of people of color, encouraging them to value whiteness and to strive toward it.

The majority of the women I interviewed painfully discussed their relationships with other women and their own feelings of inadequacy stemming from their color. They either felt that they were considered ugly because they were too dark, or they felt that they lacked substantial relationships with other women because they were too light and no one trusted them. Other women felt they were constantly being compared to lighter more beautiful women, even by their own friends and family. The most distressing commonality among the interviewees is that almost all of their pain resulting from colorism, came from the words and deeds of members of their own ethnic groups. Pamela, a dark-skinned African American woman, said,

> To tell you the truth, I didn't have many black friends in high school because in high school I was teased [about my color]. So

> I just stuck with the people who didn't really care about my skin color and that was everyone but black people.

And Elena, a lighter-skinned Mexican American, said,

> I faced what I would consider discrimination from my own people. I have also faced it from other people, but the bulk of it has been from my own community.

Both light-skinned and dark-skinned women described feeling let down by members of their own ethnic groups when they had painful experiences over skin color. Although African Americans and Mexican Americans have done their part in maintaining colorism and allowing it to enter their relationships with one another, white racism remains the root of this system.

Despite the grim situation of internalized racism in both the African American and Mexican American communities, progress has been made. Almost without exception, the great majority of the women I interviewed expressed some amount of pride in their ethnic identity. Further, many of the interviewees were engaging in reflection about how color and race have affected their own lives and what they have done to perpetuate, or work against the hierarchies. These are examples of the critical work all people must do in order to see racism and sexism more clearly which will guide them ultimately, to be able to change society.

# 6

## THE BLACKER THE BERRY

*Ethnic Legitimacy and Skin Tone*

Walter White, a black man and long-time leader of the NAACP (1931–1955), dealt with accusations of ethnic illegitimacy throughout his life. Many people, both black and white, accused him of not being "black enough," of wanting to be white, and of being out of touch with the "real" black experience. White was a very light-skinned man who could have easily passed for white if he chose to. Instead, White chose a life of leadership in the pursuit of African American civil rights, which included involvement in Afro-American organizations worldwide. Ironically, White married a white woman who looked more black than he did. The two were often harassed in public as an interracial couple, but many people thought they were seeing a white man with a black woman, not the other way around.[1] White's story is emblematic of the struggle for ethnic authenticity that many people of color face. Acceptance and rec-ognition as legitimate members of an ethnic group is important for most people. Unfortunately, this acceptance is not always granted, especially for light-skinned African Americans and Mexican Americans.

It was 1991 when the Leband Gallery at the Loyola Marymount University had a show of ten Latina artists. And in that show, they told us they wanted us to do works that reflected our personal experiences and so I did a painting. It was a self portrait. But it was called "Names Can't Hurt". It was a self portrait of me putting the make up on in the mirror but the make up is dark, is like a darker type of make up. And around the mirror frame is words that I was called throughout my childhood and growing up. Like Güera, Green Eyes, Cat Eyes, White Girl and stuff like that. I did have an identity problem for awhile there. When I grew up in the housing projects, I remember a lot of other Latinas and Chicanas telling me, ". . . you think you're better than we are because you have green eyes." And I never even thought—that never even came into my mind! And so I developed this sort of insecurity—or what is that? A complex about being light skinned . . . Maybe I became really involved in the Chicano art scene and worked with the UFW because of this desire to like prove that I'm Mexican or whatever. I don't know. . . . It felt good to do that painting [the self portrait] because I had never dealt with that issue of being a light skinned person and having seen it as a problem rather than an asset.[2]

In the story above, Barbara Carrasco, in an interview for the Smithsonian Archives of American Art, describes her own struggles with light skin tone and Chicana identity. In her own words, Carrasco shares the difficulties of being a light-skinned Chicana in Los Angeles and negotiating her role in the Chicano arts scene. *Name's Can't Hurt*, her acclaimed self-portrait, is a visual explanation of the yearning for authentic, recognized ethnic group membership. The woman in the painting is putting dark brown makeup on her light brown skin. Carrasco's story shares a theme with Walter White's: legitimacy in ethnic leadership roles. Carrasco, a leader in the Chicano Arts Movement, reflects on the complexity of her own motivations for her now famous work with the United Farm Workers. The public accomplishments and personal struggles of Carrasco and White reveal the intricate terrain of skin color politics. This chapter will explore how ethnic authenticity inverts the typical advantages of light skin. Mexican American and African American women share their own struggles with identity, group acceptance, and skin color.

## COSTS OF LIGHT-SKIN PRIVILEGE: (IN)AUTHENTICITY

Being at the front of the beauty queue offers black and Mexican American women both benefits and costs. The previous discussion highlighted the benefits that lighter women receive in terms of heterosexual dating practices and high beauty status in the eyes of both women and men. Lighter-skinned women in both the African American and Mexican American communities generally experience higher levels of beauty status than darker-skinned women and advantages in the dating/marriage market. From my interviews, however, I also discovered the *costs* to being at the front of the beauty queue. One of the costs of having light skin in these communities is having to prove oneself as an authentic or legitimate member of the ethnic community. This was true for both Mexican Americans and African Americans; issues of ethnic authenticity related to skin color were pervasive. For African American women, authenticity was the vehicle through which darker-skinned women took back their power from lighter-skinned women. Darker-skinned women often felt put down by light-skinned women and one of the most common ways they regained their power, and felt better about themselves, was to accuse light-skinned black women of not being black enough. This tactic has particular power against those lighter-skinned women who are from racially mixed backgrounds. Not being black enough, or authentically ethnic enough, in any ethnic community, is a serious insult to many. It implies that they do not identify with their fellow ethnics, that they do not care about them, and that they think they are better than their co-ethnics, or in extreme cases, that they wish they were white.

For Mexican Americans, authenticity was also a common theme in the interviews, though Mexican American women did not use it in the same way that African American women did. For Mexican Americans color was very closely associated with political views about Mexico and Chicano political consciousness. Light skin was associated with not being "Chicano enough" and not being politically affiliated enough with the Mexican or Mexican American community. From my interviews with Mexican American women, I learned that skin color is also closely associated with language where dark skin and Spanish language ability are key identifiers of Chicano identity. Conversely, light skin and "English only" skills were identified with Anglo assimilation and thus devalued in some Mexican American communities. Herein lies the contradiction: on one hand, dark skin is associated with being Indian and therefore backward and ugly, low status. On the other hand, dark skin is evidence of being Indian and therefore, of being truly or authentically *Mexicano*. The contradiction between dark skin color as low status and dark skin color as authentically ethnic is true in both communities and was an ongoing source of tension for women in almost all of the interviews. This chapter explores the cost of light skin privilege as it is experienced by women in both ethnic communities.

## WHAT DOES IT MEAN TO BE MEXICAN AMERICAN?

Jennifer is a fourth-generation Mexican American woman with very light skin. She describes herself as often inadvertently passing for white with people who do not know her because of her light skin and European features. She says that she is proud of being Mexican, although she knows little about Mexican culture and she does not speak Spanish. She spends a significant amount of time at her boyfriend's house. He is a second generation Mexican American, and she describes feeling less authentically "Hispanic" there.

> I know there have been times that because I was lighter, people thought I wasn't Hispanic enough. This happens all the time at my boyfriend's house. Everyone speaks Spanish and everything and lots of times they'll be talking about whatever and they'll say, "honkie" and then they'll say, "Oh, sorry Jennifer." And I'm like, "What are you talking about?" That happens. And one time my roommate and I were talking about speaking Spanish, because she's a Spanish major, my Caucasian roommate, and we were talking about speaking Spanish and she was like, "You're not a real Mexican, you don't speak Spanish." And I was like, "What are you talking about?" It makes me so pissed! I mean I don't judge her, how she is culturally or her ethnicity or whatever.

Jennifer is struggling with the question of what it means to be Hispanic. Her use of the term "Hispanic" instead of Latino, Chicano, or Mexican also belies her level of political consciousness in a region and on a college campus where Latino is usually used in place of Hispanic. She is sure that the fact that she has light skin adds to others' construction of her as "less Hispanic."

It is also important to note that throughout her interview, Jennifer also used several rhetorical devices to distance herself from the Mexican American community including using the word "they" as opposed to "we," and adhering to negative stereotypes about Mexican Americans. This contradiction reveals the very personal nature of ethnic identity construction. Jennifer both accepts and denies a Mexican American identity. Consequently, when her identity is questioned in any way, she feels self-doubt and resentment. As the psychologist Maria P. P. Root explains in her work on multiracial identity development, contradictory feelings about one's ethnic identity are actually quite common.[3]

Further, Jennifer's situation illustrates the close link between color, authenticity, and Spanish language ability for Mexican Americans. As much as light skin makes her a target for being less authentically Mexican, not being able to speak Spanish has a similar effect. Spanish language ability is particularly important in contexts where there are many immigrants from Mexico and Spanish language use is closely associated with being

Mexican by those both inside and outside of the Mexican American community.[4] Continued immigration from Mexico also refreshes the language use of assimilating Mexican Americans, slowing the move toward English monolingualism and encouraging bilingualism. In this context, Jennifer's inability to speak Spanish further called into question her "legitimate" claim to a Mexican American identity.

However, even light-skinned women who do speak Spanish often encounter difficulty.

> When people ask me, "What nationality are you?" I say, "I'm *Mexicana.*" "Oh, you are? Are you mixed? You're so light-skinned."...People are always amazed that I speak Spanish.

Marisel's experiences are the exception that proves the rule. The fact that she is very light-skinned and speaks Spanish was surprising to many people. Although her light skin was often a liability in being accepted as a legitimate *Mexicana*, her ability to speak Spanish helped to compensate.

Another example of the relationship between skin color, language ability, and ethnic identity was provided by Elena, a Mexican American woman who describes her relationship with her two sets of Mexican American grandparents. Elena said that as a child, she thought that she had one set of Mexican grandparents and one set of white grandparents. No one ever told her that overtly, but the meaning she derived from their skin color and language ability led her to that conclusion. She reflected on her childhood misperceptions.

> My grandparents from my mother's side...for some reason I always thought in my head, when I was a little kid, that my mom's parents, they were my Mexican grandparents and my dad's parents weren't. And I was like why did I think that when I was little? I think it's because my dad's family is very light. I don't know why, they just don't look Mexican. They're just very light. They spoke Spanish, but not as frequently as my mom's parents.

Elena's memories of constructing her grandparents' identities is illustrative of the complex interplay between color, language, and identity. Another important factor in creating a legitimate Mexican American identity for many of the women I interviewed was class. Elena recounts some of her high school and college experiences as an upper-middle-class Chicana.

Being upper-middle class and going to a [high] school where most everybody was working class or poor, that caused me a lot of problems, especially as a Chicana because I was not taken seriously. People called me a sell out... I was not taken in by any of the groups here [in college] because, number one, some people told me I did not look Chicana enough. I'm not a fluent Spanish speaker so that wasn't good enough. Other people were like, "What? You don't do work study? You don't have a job? You don't have financial aid? What's up with that?"... So we started a Latina sorority, which was really good for us because I can honestly say it's what helped me get through, but it was met with a lot of controversy. And so if I was being called a "sell out" or "whitewashed" when I first got here, you can imagine what my affiliation has caused me to have.

Elena's controversial role as a Latina sorority founder highlights the important role that social class still plays in forming an authentic Mexican American identity. Although the black middle class is also relatively small, it has a longer history and therefore more established institutions and organizations in the United States than does the middle-class Mexican American community. Although this is quickly changing, most Mexican American college students are children or grandchildren of immigrants and therefore are typically from more modest class backgrounds.

Because adolescence and early adulthood are times of identity development for most people, it makes sense that school-age experiences are central in shaping people's ethnic identities. Isabel, a Mexican American woman with darker skin, describes her experiences in elementary and high school and how her feelings about being dark-skinned changed over time.

When I was thinking about skin color, I remember that when I was younger I used to hate being dark. When I was younger, every time I went to the beach I always wanted to cover myself up because I was afraid I'd get darker and people would make fun of me. People used to always call me *morena* [dark one]. I don't know why I never really liked it. Once I got to high school I loved being dark though and I didn't really care. I think it was just a realization of who I was and being proud of who I was.

Isabel overcame her shame of being darker-skinned by connecting her dark skin to her Mexican heritage. In this case, Isabel embraced the connection between dark skin and ethnic authenticity to gain pride about her appearance and her identity as Mexican American. As they grew older, darker-skinned participants almost uniformly gained ethnic pride and a sense of belonging from their skin color. Many reported feeling a part of the group, especially in ethnic organizations in high school or college. These stories exemplify one of the benefits of dark skin–ethnic legitimacy.

Brown skin and indigenous features are a source of Chicano pride in many circles. Catalina, a light-skinned Mexican American, describes an argument she had with a former boyfriend about dying her hair.

> My ex-boyfriend, he was really into Latino stuff. I remember I would tell him that I was going to dye my hair . . . and he got kind of mad and said, "I like your hair black, the way it is." . . . He would tell me that it just looks fake and trying to be somebody who I really wasn't. I don't see how your hair color could really change who you are. Plus, I was telling him that I wanted to try colored contacts. And he told me that black eyes were beautiful the way they were and I didn't need to be another person. He started to tell me that if I wore blue contacts that I was saying that blue eyes were better than my natural colored eyes. I just really didn't see it that way. It's just a different color. It's not changing my own person. . . . Maybe that was what broke it off, though I never changed the color. He was a lot into being Latino.

Catalina's discussion with her boyfriend reveals the complex dynamic between skin color, facial features and ethnic pride. Catalina wanted to experiment with changes to her appearance and her boyfriend interpreted those changes as assaults against her ethnic identity. Perhaps Catalina wanted to lighten her hair and eyes to gain more status in the beauty queue, or to get more social capital through beauty. Whatever her motivations, the idea of lightening her appearance raised prickly issues for her boyfriend who located Latino pride, at least partially, in physical appearance.

Because many of the interviewees were college students, ethnic student organizations were a common topic of discussion. Criteria for membership in these organizations were sometimes overt, but often unspoken. Several participants described informal rules about skin color and language ability that affected acceptance into these organizations. Marisel, a light-skinned Mexican American woman, was born in Mexico and raised in the United States. She describes her dismay about the practices of the Chicano Student Organization (CSO) on her university campus.

> It seems like you have to have a certain look to be in CSO, indigenous or something. To make sure you prove yourself—that you're *Mexicano*. So in that aspect they do look at skin color. Because what if I walk in? I'm 100% *Mexicana*, but what if they treat me badly because I'm light-skinned? Like they say, "What are you doing here?" They shouldn't be that way, based on how you look. Not on skin color. That doesn't take anything away from me being *Mexicana* or what I can do for the Chicano community.

Marisel's insistence that her light skin is not a liability in terms of authenticity is a reaction to an implicit assumption that it is. Marisel raises another interesting point. She states unequivocally that her light skin does not make her less politically engaged or less race-conscious as a Chicana. Her opinion was echoed in interviews with several other light-skinned women from both communities. For example, a light-skinned African American woman expresses concern about joining the African American Student Organization (AASO) on campus.

> I really feel like I'm not accepted by the black community here [at this university]. I mean if I wanted to go to AASO or something, I'm sure they'd try to be nice, but I just feel like it would be a really scary thing.

Linda, a light-skinned Mexican American, describes her confusion and frustration about the perceptions of light-skinned people as sell outs.

> You have your advantages if you're lighter...So they have certain privileges that other people don't. Maybe that's like society as a whole, but when it comes to your own group, if you are lighter then it's like you're one of them [white people]. Or you might be trying to be one of them [white people]. You're a sell out...So, it's like you're caught in between...I'm kind of rejected by my own group...Maybe that's why I'm trying to like find out where I'm supposed to go. I don't know what I'm supposed to do sometimes. Like who am I supposed to go to, you know?

Many of the light-skinned African American and Mexican American women expressed frustration and fear about joining race-based student organizations. Although they thought they had much to offer and many considered themselves race-conscious, they either felt rebuffed or anticipated feeling rebuffed by co-ethnics because of their light skin.

Interestingly, the contention that light skin does not make one less Chicano, or less black when defined as less race-conscious, is at odds with much sociological research.

The majority of research on skin color and racial attitudes among both Mexican American and African Americans is consistent: light-skinned people tend to be less identified with their ethnic communities, tend to have less ethnic pride, and tend to be less radical about racial issues than their dark-skinned counterparts.[5] This means that light-skinned people are less likely to think racial discrimination is a serious problem for people of color and they are less likely to believe in more radical racial politics like separatism or cultural nationalism.

The discrepancy between the feelings of many light-skinned interviewees and the sociological research findings raises a perplexing contradiction. Although the majority of the light-skinned women that I interviewed felt similarly to Marisel, most were aware of the prevailing notion that darker skin is a symbol of increased racial consciousness. The beliefs of the women I interviewed offer some counter evidence to the prevailing theory that light skin makes for a weak ethnic identity. However, there are several possible reasons why my findings differed from those of most other studies. First, my interview sample was self-selected, therefore the women who participated may be more politically inclined and thus more interested in participating in research about racial politics. Second, my interviewees were college students and consequently more likely to be politically involved and aware of race relations in the United States. Third, I think it is very possible that a social desirability bias was at work with this issue. Although light-skinned people of color may be less racially conscious and have weaker ethnic identities than their darker-skinned counterparts, it is not politically correct to be considered a sell out, therefore the light-skinned people I interviewed might be inclined to exaggerate their political stances on racial issues in order to seem more racially conscious than they really are. Ideally, more research will be done in this area to help sort out these complexities.

Isabel confirms the theory that darker-skinned people are more strongly ethnically identified and seen as more ethnically authentic. I asked Isabel, a dark-skinned Mexican American, if she believes that Chicanos at her university think darker skin means a more legitimate Chicano identity.

> I think here [the university] there is a favoritism of darker. If you speak Spanish you're favored because it is a characteristic of being Mexican. So I think being darker is favored because it is a characteristic of being Mexican. So if you're lighter you resemble

white....I don't think that's good, but I think that darker is favored. Partly because there is so much Chicano pride here.

Clearly, there is a connection among dark skin, Spanish language
ability, and being considered ethnically Mexican. It is important to note,
however, that none of the participants argued that darker skin was considered more beautiful, simply that it was considered more Mexican.

The statements of all of these women support the idea that in some
limited contexts, particularly those where ethnic identity and legitimacy
were at stake, it is considered positive to be darker-skinned. In general, the
women acknowledged that light skin was extremely desirable, with the
notable exception of ethnic group membership. For Mexican Americans,
the enduring importance of skin color, and the overwhelming belief
that darker skin is not desirable is at odds with the Mexican ideology
of *mestizaje*. *Mestizaje* is an ideology widely held throughout Latin
America that purports race-mixing as a means to a new and inclusive
hybrid national identity. *Mestizaje* means "mixture" and refers to the
history of intermarriage and miscegenation in Mexico that created a
new, mixed race of people who transcend color and caste. The ideology
of *mestizaje* is a powerful one that overlooks racial and color differences
and focuses on the commonalities among all Mexicans.[6] Even though
this is a dominant ideology throughout Latin America, it is in conflict
with the reality of an ongoing color-caste system left over from the colonial rule of Spain and the influence of the United States. It is the belief
in *mestizaje* that makes it difficult for many Mexicans to discuss racial
or color discrimination in Mexico at all. It is often seen as an American
problem, because in Mexico everyone, regardless of color, is considered
Mexican. Although the ideology of *mestizaje* has a firm hold in the
minds of many Mexicans and Mexican Americans, one need only look
at the class differences among the lighter and darker-skinned Mexicans
both in Mexico and here in the United States to see the ongoing effects
of colonialism and racism.

The light-skinned participants were clear that dark skin color was
definitely an advantage when it came to issues of ethnic identity and
legitimacy. Many light-skinned Mexican Americans expressed pain,
frustration, and disappointment at being excluded from ethnic organizations and generally being regarded as less than full members of the
Mexican American community. However, despite their strong feelings,
it is compelling to note that not one of the light-skinned participants
suggested that she wanted to be darker-skinned. Despite the negative con-
notations of light skin and the alienation they often felt, the advantages
of light skin clearly outweighed the disadvantages for these women as

none stated that she ever wished she were darker. Additionally, almost all of the dark-skinned women expressed feeling, at some time in their lives, the yearning to be lighter. These findings are central to the argument I am making because they highlight the complexity of skin color politics within ethnic communities, while also demonstrating the strong and enduring privilege of light skin. Although the pull to be seen as an authentic and legitimate member of one's community is strong, the privileges of light skin are even stronger.

Although most of the light-skinned Mexican American women reported strong senses of ethnic identity, there was one clear example of a light-skinned person who was not particularly interested in being an active member of the Mexican American community. In my interview with Diana, a light-skinned woman who could probably pass for white, she consistently tried to distance herself from other Latinos.

> I've never had any Hispanic friends. All my friends were white or Asian. I always felt that was really weird. And there have been times when I almost got my butt kicked because I wasn't Hispanic enough. I still get stuff like, "Oh, she thinks she's white." And I'm like, "No. I know what I am." My friend Tina called me whitewashed the other day. How does a white person get off calling me whitewashed? And then Justin, my boyfriend last year, broke up with me because he thought I wasn't Hispanic enough. [MH: Was he Hispanic?] No! That's the insane part! But all his friends were. I met his friends and I had absolutely nothing to say to them. I thought they were a bunch of losers and I could not wait to leave. He asked me, "Are you ashamed of being Hispanic? You never speak Spanish. You don't have any Hispanic friends." I'm like what, "Because I don't have my permed hair, and the red lipstick?"

Diana reacts with shock and incredulity when she is accused of acting white by white people in her life. She is surprised to be considered "not Hispanic enough," yet she simultaneously distances herself from Latinos.[7] Her distancing is evidenced in her description of her boyfriend's Hispanic friends as "a bunch of losers." In other references to Latinos throughout the interview she continually relied on racist stereotypes and described how she was different from them. Also, she invokes a stereotype of Latina women having permed hair and wearing red lipstick. She mocks and denigrates this identity and again distances herself from it by pointing out that she does not do her hair and make-up that way.

Diana's discussion of her identity as Mexican American reveals an existential question about identity—what does it mean to *be* Mexican

American? Diana does not wish to identify as white, yet she consistently distances herself from other ethnic group members. Her behavior fits the stereotype of light-skinned people not wanting to identify as Mexican and justifies biases, as were discussed above, toward constructing darker-skinned people as more politically affiliated with the Chicano population. Diana's case raises interesting questions about authenticity, color, and group membership and makes one wonder if she is the exception or the rule.

Perhaps what is most provocative about darker-skinned people being identified as more authentic, is the paradox it presents for light-skin privilege. On one hand, light-skinned Mexican American women are constantly being elevated in status as *las güeras* and given privileges both inside and outside of the Mexican American community. On the other hand, darker-skinned people are favored within the Mexican American community, but only in the sense that they are considered truly Mexican because of their more Indian appearance. This seeming paradox draws on the ideology of *mestizaje*, as well as the vestiges of the Spanish racial order.

## IF BLACK ISN'T BEAUTIFUL, AT LEAST IT'S AUTHENTIC

Mexican Americans were not alone in their dilemmas with ethnic legitimacy. The interviews with African American women revealed that ethnic authenticity was an equally important issue for them. Predictably, the lighter members of the African American community were most likely to be accused of being not black enough. Many African Americans consider light-skinned members of the community to be less identified with other blacks and less interested in and knowledgeable about black culture, a presumption that is consistent with much of the social science research on this topic.

The irony however, is that the members who are seen as the least identified with the black community, the lightest-skinned people, are also the ones elevated to the status of most beautiful and most desirable by African American men.

Regina, a light-skinned African American woman, told me about her experiences in a private high school where she was part of a small, close knit group of black students. She reports feeling marginalized in this group.

> I still felt though, being as light as I was, I still felt that I wasn't completely accepted. There was still something there. It never bothered me though. I didn't care because I'm very confident

with myself and I don't care what they think about me. They used to call me, "white girl." Just subtle things like that. When they'd be saying something they'd ask, "Do you need us to clarify that for you? Ha ha." About black culture kinds of stuff. It was always taken as a joke, but it started to get on my nerves to the point where I would say, "Will you stop calling me that? I hate when you say that."

Regina's classmates continually drew boundaries around blackness, purposefully excluding her and reminding her that she was different from them—more white. The meaning of light skin takes on an added twist when it is coupled with the liability of being seen as a disloyal ethnic group member, or in this case, not a true member at all. Regina's light skin was a signifier of whiteness, and Regina was regularly reminded by her black counterparts that she was not a legitimate member of the group. It is also useful to speculate about why her black peers worked so hard to continually draw these racial boundaries. What did they get out of it? It is possible that Regina's light skin and the privileges that go with it reinforce the other black students' sense of racial stigma. The antidote to the stigma is to exclude the light-skinned person from something of worth—in this case, black culture. Regina's experiences were emblematic of those of other light-skinned interviewees who reported feeling isolated from other black students and constantly reminded that they were not full members of the black community.

Tisha, one of the few women I interviewed who is a mother, describes her concerns about raising her light-skinned son.

> Well, I do have to deal with the whole issue of my son being pretty light.... When I met my husband, people were like, "Oh, your babies are going to have real good hair." That's like the least of my worries. First, I have to raise a black man, first and foremost. It'll be important for me to let him know he's not any better because of his color... And I'm going to warn him that, "All those little girls are going to want you because of your hair and your color, but we all struggling and when it comes down to it, you just as black as the blackest person." That's important for me to get across to him.

Tisha already anticipates her son's potential to feel superior to other African Americans because of his skin color. Even though her son was quite young at the time of the interview, her desire to let him know that he is "as black as the blackest person" shows her awareness that skin color may be a barrier to an authentic black identity. Her warning also belies an assumption that light skin color produces a superiority complex, one that she wants to nip in the bud for her son.

Other black women I spoke with suggested that light-skinned people sometimes associated with dark-skinned people in order to prove their blackness. Maya, a brown-skinned woman, describes her sister's experiences.

> My sister, who is much lighter than me, they say she's not even black. She looks Puerto Rican. All of her friends are black. Some people say she's just acting black to make sure people know she's black.

Maya's description of her sister's experiences demonstrates the paradoxical nature of color and ethnic identity. Maya's sister has to "act black" by having exclusively black friends, in order to show to others that she "really is black." In this way, the performance of blackness is more important than the familial ties of blackness. It is not enough to simply "be black." One must also perform blackness to communicate her blackness to others, especially if it might be questioned because of skin tone.[8] This seeming paradox of color and authenticity was echoed by other black women. Belinda, an African American woman with dark brown skin, describes her surprise and then skepticism about the role of light-skinned students in the African American Student Organization (AASO) on her university campus.

> Here at our university it seems like a lot of light-skinned people are really the activists. Like the leaders of AASO are light, with kind of wavy hair. They're not just blue-black you know. One of the women who was really active in the Affirmative Action stuff is really light...and then you wonder what they're in it for. Is she trying to prove her blackness? Is that why she's kind of in the mix with all of the AASO black people?

The theme of light-skinned African Americans as less politically aligned with the African American community is clear in Belinda's words. In fact, she expresses some surprise that the leaders of the African American Student Organization are not "blue black"—a potentially demeaning way to describe very dark skin and further evidence that many believe that darker-skinned people are more politically active in racial issues than others. Belinda's observation that many light-skinned students are leaders of the AASO conflicts with her beliefs about light-skinned people as not politically active in black issues, so she inverts the situation and wonders aloud if their participation in this organization is not for the betterment of black people, but instead is to prove publicly that they really are "black enough." This would turn their motivations from group oriented and altruistic, to selfish and individualistic.

The complex relationship between skin color and race consciousness is not a new phenomenon. Although it is true that survey research reveals weaker ethnic identities and weaker group ties among light-skinned and upper class black people, it is also true that many influential African American leaders have been light-skinned.[9] W. E. B. Du Bois, a founder of the NAACP and a highly influential black leader for decades, was also very light-skinned. Julian Bond, Adam Clayton Powell, Malcolm X and others have also been light-skinned. In fact, it was so common for black leaders to be light-skinned, that Marcus Garvey's popularity was believed to be due, in part, to his dark skin color. Garvey was a powerful orator and organizer of black economic self-sufficiency, black pride, and he spearheaded a movement back to Africa.

One of the reasons that so many African American civil rights leaders have been light-skinned is because of the history of colorism in black organizations. Many elite black organizations have had color tests that potential members had to pass for membership. The most infamous of these tests was the brown bag test. This test required that a person's skin color be lighter than a brown paper bag for entrance. Many black fraternities and sororities were notorious for admitting only light-skinned people; this is still true for some today. Even some black churches that had upper-class congregants would discourage dark-skinned worshippers from attending services there. This kind of color-based gatekeeping in elite organizations gave light-skinned people a distinct advantage in terms of education and social networks.[10] Despite larger trends of dark-skinned people with higher levels of commitment to their communities, the history of black civil rights leaders includes a disproportionate number of light-skinned men and women.

Ethnic authenticity is not just centered around politics. It also is strongly related to culture, as was evidenced by the Mexican American concern for speaking Spanish. Among African Americans, dark skin may also be associated with African and African American culture. Delilah, an African American interviewee, describes why she thinks that black women are more interested in dark-skinned rather than lighter-skinned black men.

> Before, I think black women used to go for the lighter guys, but now I think they go for more of the darker. The way I hear them

talk about it is that they like the darker guys, that that's what makes them sexy or attractive. The darker guys seem more tied down to where they came from. They might wear African attire, not that they are necessarily from Africa. It's usually the darker-skinned men who wear the African jewelry, walk around with a cane, that wear the traditional African outfits. Like, when they see a black woman they'll say, "Hi my beautiful black sister." They'll come out like that. A lot of black women like that because I think they feel they're being put up on a pedestal, like they're being picked out. Most of the light-skinned guys, since they tend to be mixed, most of the ones I've seen don't tend to be as Afrocentric.

Delilah explained that dark-skinned men are more likely to be Afrocentric than light-skinned men because many light-skinned men are racially mixed, and therefore presumably less connected to the black community and black people. Conversely, dark-skinned black men are characterized as not only more authentically black, but also more affirming of black culture and aesthetics, especially dark skin. Delilah seems to be arguing that light-skinned men are not reliably black-affirming, and therefore may be hostile toward or disinterested in dark-skinned black women. For many black women then, darker-skinned men are more trustworthy and more authentic, than light. According to Delilah, praising the natural Afrocentric beauty of black women is a positive trait in many men, even if it is not typical.

Delilah's comments are very important to this discussion for two reasons. First, she confirms the stereotype that dark-skinned men are more authentically black and that light-skinned men are not "black enough." Second, she inadvertently highlights the gender difference in the value of skin color. She does not mention darker-skinned black women as elevated to a higher status for being more ethnic, as black men are. In fact, it seems that for men there is more mobility around issues of status and skin color than there is for women. By this, I mean that for men there are times when it may be beneficial to be dark-skinned and there may be social rewards for being so. Conversely, for women, there seems to be almost no time when it is more socially desirable to be dark-skinned.

Delilah's description of light-skinned African American men as more interested in light-skinned women was confirmed by Belinda, a dark-skinned African American woman. Belinda told me about how difficult it is to think clearly about issues of color. Colorism is such a touchy subject in the black community and is so bound up in issues of self-esteem and status that sorting out one's perceptions from reality can be very difficult.

I was at this party once and I saw the guy that I liked dancing with all these girls and they were all light or mixed. And at first I thought, "Oh see he just wants to be with a light-skinned girl. He's got a color complex. He's colorstruck." But then I thought, maybe those are the girls who just happened to walk up to him. Like they are the ones who happened to approach him. That could be. So then I thought, maybe I'm the one who's colorstruck for even thinking about it in the first place. Like maybe I'm the one with the problem.

Belinda's thoughts to herself are an example of how much skin color structures the world of heterosexual relationships for African American and Mexican American women. Belinda inverts her initial accusation that the light-skinned man is "colorstruck" and turns it around on herself, to wonder if she is the one overly concerned with color. To be called "colorstruck" in the African American community is an insult. It means that a person is consumed with issues of color and, usually, that the person has a preference for light skin (in herself or others). To be considered colorstruck is to be seen as superficial or even stuck up. Belinda believes that because she is thinking about color and assuming the privilege of the light-skinned women over her, that perhaps she is the one who is consumed with color and status. Given the patterns of social interaction, it is not likely that what Belinda witnessed was a random choice of the women and men involved. It is common to see men of any color, and particularly light-skinned men, choose light-skinned women for dating and marriage. Belinda's ruminations over this incident and over her beliefs about skin color in general demonstrate how complicated this issue can be.

## IS THE GRASS ALWAYS GREENER ON THE OTHER SIDE?

One could characterize the problem of colorism as equally difficult for both light-and dark-skinned people. Dark-skinned women lack the social capital that light skin provides, and are therefore disadvantaged in education and employment. Additionally, dark skin is generally not regarded as beautiful, so dark-skinned women often lose out in the dating and marriage markets. On the other side, light-skinned men and women are typically not regarded as legitimate members of the African American or Mexican American communities. They may be excluded from or made to feel unwelcome in community events and organizations. At first glance, it may seem that there are equal advantages and disadvantages to both sides of the color line. Upon closer examination, this proves to be untrue. Although exclusion from some community organizations may be uncomfortable psychologically or emotionally for light-skinned people of color, it rarely has significant material effects. More specifically, emotional turmoil about ethnic identity does not have significant economic consequences. However, the systematic discrimination against dark-skinned people of color in the labor market, educational institutions, and marriage market create marked economic disadvantages. Without minimizing the psychological trauma of exclusion from ethnic communities, it is important to clarify that the disadvantages of dark skin still far outweigh the disadvantages of light.

When compared in this way, it is not simply a case of "the grass is always greener on the other side." Although there are downsides to both ends of the color spectrum, the penalties are more common and more severe for dark skin than for light. This is evidenced by the following observation from my interviews. Nearly all of the dark-skinned women wanted to be lighter at some time in their lives in order to accrue some of the privileges of light skin. In contrast, despite the painful stories of exclusion from many light-skinned women, none reported ever wanting to be darker-skinned. This significant difference points to the enduring and substantial privilege of light skin.

# 7

## COLOR AND THE CHANGING
## RACIAL LANDSCAPE

Skin color remains an important factor in social life today. Qualitative interviews with the author, as well as nearly two thousand cases of survey data have all provided evidence to this fact. However, some may wonder if things have changed since the survey data was collected over twenty years ago. No similar comprehensive national study has been done since, but recent, smaller studies suggest that dark skin color remains a strong liability for Mexican Americans and African Americans. For example, in 2000, Mark Hill, in his study of African American men, found that skin tone accounted for more differences in social status among the men than family background did. Light-skinned black men retained a significant advantage in the labor market.[1] In 2002, Rodolfo Espino and Michael Franz studied skin color differences among Latinos. They wrote, "Our findings indicate that darker-skinned Mexicans and Cubans face significantly lower occupational prestige scores than their lighter-skinned counterparts even when controlling for factors that influence performance in the labor market."[2] Skin tone bias remains persistent over the years and across racial groups. In 2003, *The Washington Post* reported that Latinos who identified as white earned about $5,000 more per year than Latinos who identified as black. White Latinos had lower unemployment rates and lower poverty rates than black Latinos.[3] In a similar analysis, Richard Alba, John Logan, and Brian Stults reported that, "Hispanics who describe themselves as black are in substantially poorer and less white neighborhoods than their compatriots who describe themselves as white. The penalty they absorb in neighborhood affluence

111

varies between $3,500 and $6,000 and thus places them in neighborhoods comparable to those occupied by African Americans.["]4 All of these studies published in the past few years reveal that discrimination by skin tone has not eased for Mexican Americans and African Americans. Lighter skin still buys more privileges and dark skin remains a liability in work, housing, and education.

## A RACIAL LATIN AMERICANIZATION?

Skin color mattered in the past and it matters today. It affects how much money people make, how long they stay in school, who they think is pretty, who they marry, and what kind of racial identity they have. But the racial landscape in the United States is changing everyday. How will color matter in the future? Noted sociologist Eduardo Bonilla-Silva contends that the United States is in a process of racial "Latin Americanization."[5] As the United States moves more and more toward a colorblind discourse, one that does not acknowledge racial difference or racial inequality, it begins to mirror the historical trend in much of Latin America that denies race and insists on a national identity. It is popular in Mexico, for example, to say that there are no races like in the United States; there are only Mexicans. And this is true to some extent. Mexico does not have a U.S.-style racial system, but it definitely has distinct differences by ancestry, some more indigenous or African, some more Spanish, and they have a full spectrum of colors from dark to light. And even though they do not "do race" the way their northern neighbors do, the pattern looks notoriously similar: a light-skinned elite and a disenfranchised dark-skinned underclass.

The United States is going through a racial Latin Americanization because its discourse has changed in this post-civil rights era to one that denies difference, denies inequality, and insists on a unified, monolithic American designation for all.[6] This colorblind discourse makes it possible to ignore racial discrimination and to criticize those who name it as racist for doing so.[7] Several recent political movements reflect this trend. The national backlash against Affirmative Action is one example.[8] What began in California as a statewide referendum to abolish Affirmative Action in state-regulated affairs in 1996 culminated in the University of Michigan's U.S. Supreme Court cases defending its use of Affirmative Action. In two related cases, the University won the right to use race as one criterion that could be considered in university admissions.[9] The University of Michigan battle revealed the changing contours of race-talk in the United States. The plaintiffs argued that a colorblind society was desirable and could only be achieved by ignoring race in admission decisions. Affirmative Action had to be dismantled, they argued, in order to create a non-racist society. The defendants argued, among other things, that Affirmative Action was still necessary to combat persistent discrimination and inequality, and that a racially diverse student body was academically beneficial to all students.

It is the same colorblind ideology that led University of California Regent Ward Connerly to lead a campaign supporting the Racial Privacy Initiative[10] in California in 2002. This state initiative would have made it illegal for the state of California to collect any data on race and ethnicity including data regarding housing, education, and employment. A colorblind society would require that we not take note of any person's race, supporters have argued. The fact that racial discrimination and inequality would become impossible to monitor and easier to get away with never entered the public debate. This initiative was voted down by Californians largely because of a campaign warning that important medical information that varies by race would be unavailable if the act passed.[11]

Many Latin American countries have avoided collecting racial data for years. Puerto Rico recently, began collecting data on the race of its residents. Similarly, Brazil is just beginning to collect some statistics on the different standards of living of Afro-Brazilians, mulattoes, and white Brazilians. Thus, as the United States becomes more like Latin America and pretends racism is not a problem, parts of Latin America are changing to emulate the traditions of the United States. Brazil initiated its first Affirmative Action program regulating admission to the elite public university system.[12] This movement is connected to a small, but growing Afro-Brazilian movement that champions black pride and identity and names racism and inequality while the rest of the nation chants "racial democracy."[13] The program has been met with fierce resistance, especially from elite white families who are no longer guaranteed the admissions to universities they once were. In some Latin American societies, race is becoming a local vocabulary word, not one only imported from the United States. As poverty becomes more entrenched among the dark-skinned poor and money and political power continue to reside strictly in the hands of a light-skinned elite, the deafening silence about racial inequality will be increasingly difficult to maintain.

In addition to a change in racial ideology and discourse, the United States is also becoming more Latin American in terms of demographics. People identifying as Hispanic on the U.S. Census now outnumber the number of people identifying as solely black or African American. In a typically sensational manner, the mainstream American media covered the event as a sort of racial boxing match. Latinos versus blacks: the battle of the minorities. Newspapers used words like "overtake," "left behind," "dominate," and "surpass" to describe the racial and ethnic changes in the population. Despite the superficial coverage of this demographic shift, some major changes are at work in today's racial politics. The number of Latinos in the United States is growing rapidly, although whether Latinos "outnumber" blacks depends in part on how you count. The fact that "Hispanic" is regarded as an ethnicity and all Hispanic people must also choose a race on the Census form makes counting people difficult and controversial.[14] Whether or not Latinos are now the largest ethnic minority group is not the most important issue for this argument. Latinos constitute a significant group in the United States and the presence of Latin American, particularly Mexican, culture, values, and politics is changing the U.S. racial landscape. The history of conquest in Mexico, the Chicano student movement, the fluid nature of race, and the importance of skin tone in Mexico all influence the way Americans will be rethinking race in the coming years. All of these changes beg the question: How will the growing Latino presence change the nature of U.S. race relations?

In many Latin American countries, the fluidity of race and racial categories is further complicated by the tradition that "money whitens." This phrase refers to the trend where dark-skinned people may be treated as if they are white, or allowed into some white social circles, if they are wealthy. This phenomenon has long existed in Latin America in part because they have never had the rigid distinctions of race guided by ancestry and the Rule of Hypodescent so present in the United States. For many generations, African Americans could be rich and famous, and still be guaranteed second-class status through rigid laws and rules of racial etiquette. Any famous African American performer before the Civil Rights Movement can tell stories of having to enter through the back door of establishments where she or he was going to perform to white audiences. However, since the Civil Rights Movement significant African American and Mexican American middle classes have been established and some of those people of color are quite assimilated into white social worlds.

Will the United States' turn toward a colorblind discourse allow the money whitens thesis to work here? Some would argue that it has already happened and that some people of color who are wealthy are allowed into elite white social circles. Largely, though, this is not the case. However, it may be possible in the future for dark-skinned people of color to compensate for their dark skin with wealth or high social status. This may be happening for men already. It seems that dark skin color for men is significantly mediated by wealth or social status. This may also be a function of the fact that skin color has always been more important in the evaluation of women than men.

The other way that skin color politics may play out in the future is through an "ideology whitens" hypothesis. It is possible that besides money, dark-skinned people of color may be allowed into positions of power if they are not ideologically threatening. That is, if they adopt the racial and cultural ideologies of the dominant group, their dark skin can be compensated for with conservative values. For instance, a dark-skinned Mexican American man might be able to run for governor of California if he is a Republican. In this way, his dark skin, a reminder of a potentially strong Mexican American identity, can be compensated for with a conservative political ideology. This process may already be at work in some political campaigns. Cruz Bustamante, a Democratic candidate for governor in the historic gubernatorial recall election of 2003, was dogged by accusations of being a political radical because of his membership in MEChA (Movimiento Estudiantil Chicano de Aztlán) during his undergraduate college years.[15] Bustamante, a political moderate by nearly all accounts, was forced to prove that he neither hated whites nor wanted to return California to Mexico. Bustamante's ethnic identity, phenotype, and moderately liberal political position contributed to his unsuccessful bid for governorship. Although most candidates had little chance against the action-hero celebrity Arnold Schwarzenegger, criticisms against Bustamante were overtly racial in nature. As the Republican Party continues to court people of color, it will be interesting to see if Mexican American and African American candidates will have success espousing more conservative political agendas.

The United States is currently undergoing a substantial wave of immigration primarily from third world nations. The number of immigrants from Asia and Latin America is higher than it has ever been before. The large numbers of nonwhite people moving into the United States is bound to affect the meanings of skin color and race in upcoming generations. First, immigrants come to the United States with their own racial ideologies formed in their homelands and informed by Western imperialism. Because of Western media exports, many immigrants come to the United States with well-formed negative stereotypes about African Americans. Many new immigrants face high levels of racial discrimination when they arrive here. One strategy to combat that discrimination is to align oneself with the dominant group by discriminating against other racial and ethnic minorities. Both the Jewish and the Irish immigrants did this in the 1920s when they were trying to show white Anglos that they were more like them than they were like blacks. Many Irish workers banned African Americans from their unions and Jewish performers worked in the minstrel shows, put on blackface and imitated a racist version of black life. By taking up white racist practices, these earlier immigrant groups helped construct themselves as white and not black.

Immigrants today use some of the same strategies to align themselves with dominant whites and to draw clear boundaries between themselves and other minority groups. Sometimes this happens in daily interactions, for instance, between Korean storeowners and black customers. "Studies on Korean shopkeepers in various locales have found that over 70% of them hold anti-Black attitudes."[16] There are also high profile events like the 1992 uprisings in Los Angeles that create allies of some groups and enemies of others. Asian immigrants were portrayed as innocent victims picked on by black and Latino criminals. All of these different opportunities, both mundane and monumental, provide opportunities for different racial groups to align themselves with and against other groups and to create new meanings of race and racism.

## A NEW MIDDLEMAN MINORITY?

Despite some persistent animosity among racial groups, changes in attitudes and social structures have created a growing number of inter-racial couples and multiracial people. All of this race-mixing has created a growing class of light brown people who do not readily identify with any one particular racial or ethnic group. It is possible that within one or two generations, the United States may have created a new middleman minority–a sort of light-skinned mulatto class that serves as a buffer zone between dominant whites and oppressed racial and ethnic minorities. Currently, the multiracial identity movement, led largely by white mothers of mixed race children, has advocated that multiracial individuals be allowed to simply be individuals (de-raced), or to be members of multiple ethnic groups.[17] The language of this movement borrows heavily from the new colorblind ideology. Because they are often light-skinned, many multiracial people who are part African American or Mexican American report feeling alienated from other members of their groups. The lack of ethnic authenticity leaves many multiracial people to interact only in white social circles or to feel like their only black or Mexican American friends are their own cousins, siblings, and other family members.

> Growing up, I never had any black friends or anything. Part of it was because we come from this white neighborhood and like my school was almost all white, too. But at the same time there

were black girls at school and I was totally shunned by all of them. So the only black people I felt like I could ever be a part of were my dad's side of the family because they never make me feel like, "Hey, you're not one of us." Where around anyone else, even here at [college] I feel like I'm on the outside. So my family is like really accepting.

I've always wanted to be closer with more black females, just to widen the variety a little bit more. Like if I was to go anywhere with somebody who was going to be black, it would be my cousin. I would like the liveliness, too, but to me it was just too difficult and just too much drama to be getting past the whole stereotype issue. I get it from my cousin and she's blood. She'll tease me about light skin and being white or whatever.

These biracial African American women describe their alienation from the black community because of their light skin color. The only interactions they have with other black women are restricted to their own family members where one reports, "I get it from my cousin and she's blood." There are two forces at work here. On one hand, light-skinned people, especially biracial, are sometimes excluded from relationships in the black community. On the other hand, some multiracial families, as described in the first quote, choose to remain outside of black communities and do not provide many opportunities for biracial African American children to interact with other blacks. If these trends continue, it is possible that the United States may create new kind of middleman minority comprised of light-skinned, mixed-race people who do not feel comfortable with or accepted by whites or other people of color. This new mulatto class could exist as a sort of buffer zone between white elites and oppressed racial and ethnic minorities. Bonilla-Silva agrees, "As a tri-racial system (or Latin- or Caribbean-like racial order), race conflict will be buffered by the intermediate group, much like class conflict is when the class structure includes a large middle class (Bottomore, 1968). Furthermore, color gradations, which have always been important matters of within-group differentiation, will become more salient factors of stratification."[20] If Bonilla-Silva's projections are correct, colorism will intensify and light-skinned, mixed-race individuals may have even more incentive to flee communities of color.

Historically, mixed-race people have largely been assimilated into the lower status racial group. Black-white children typically identify as black and Latino-white children often identify as Latino, especially if the Latino parent is dark-skinned. This pattern is beginning to change. As racial boundaries are questioned and the colorblind ideology of individuality dominates our culture, more and more people try to opt out of race altogether. Noted sociologist Kerry Ann Rockquemore describes this phenomenon as choosing a transcendent identity.

> These individuals discount race as a 'master status' altogether. This self-understanding is uniquely and exclusively available to individuals whose bodily characteristics have a high degree of ambiguity (i.e., those who look White). This type of self-understanding of biracialness results in an avoidance, or rejection of any type of racial group categorization as the basis of personal identity.[21]

Rockquemore articulates a new racial option for very light-skinned mixed race people: opting out of race altogether. Historically, this was impossible unless one led a deceptive life and purposefully passed for white. Today, under the ideology of colorblindness, biracial people who choose a transcendent identity are in fact choosing a white identity because they crave the invisibility of whiteness and the lack of racial demarcation that only whites enjoy. If colorism continues to plague the nation, and light-skinned multiracial people do not identify with communities of color, there is an increasing chance that the U.S. racial system will indeed become more Latin American with dominant whites, a light-skinned, mulatto intermediate group, and oppressed racial and ethnic minorities.

In order to avoid further racial polarization and to better understand the dynamics of colorism, more research must be done on other societies. This book linked colorism today to the history of slavery for African Americans and colonization for Mexican Americans. How do other postcolonial nations experience colorism? India has a very strong color-caste system, although official sources will deny it. From a legacy of British imperialism and India's own caste system, the strong value of light skin and extreme denigration of dark skin is still an aspect of daily life. And as is true in the United States, light skin color for women and girls is even more important than it is for men and boys. Similarly, the legacy of Spanish colonialism in the Philippines has left the population awash in Eurocentric values. Longer noses, and light skin are highly valued physical traits. *Mestizas*, mixed race (half white) Filipinos are often local beauty queens and national celebrities. Colorism is not a strictly American phenomenon and further investigation into how colorism operates in other postcolonial societies will expand our understanding of the issue.

In addition to studying colorism in postcolonial settings, it is also important to understand how white skin came to be revered in cultures that were never colonized by whites. In Japan, for instance, white or light skin tone is viewed as the most beautiful. How did this come to be? Is the Japanese love for white skin related to Western domination in the world and the exporting of Western images of beauty and culture? Perhaps there are parts of Japanese cultural history that explain the valorization of white skin. These are the kinds of questions researchers must ask, and answer as the problem of colorism is slowly unwound.

## THE FEMINIZATION OF COLOR

Although this book was comprehensive in covering the many ways that skin tone affects the life experiences of Mexican American and African American women, one of the omissions in this study is the experience of lesbians. Although the survey data surely included some lesbians in the nearly two thousand cases they included, none of the married women were likely lesbians, or at least living their lives as lesbians.[22] Similarly, none of the women in the qualitative portion of this study revealed to me that they were lesbians.[23] This presents a limitation of the data. This is important because much of the ado about colorism among women has to do with the evaluation of women's skin color by men. And though lesbians are not completely excluded from that they may be less influenced by, or less vulnerable to, evaluations by male peers because they are not looking for male romantic partners. Black and Chicana lesbians are still socialized in black and Chicano communities so they presumably learn the same lessons about colorism that their heterosexual peers do. However, if as adults, lesbians of color are less likely to worry about male judgments of skin tone, then how do they negotiate colorism differently?

Answers to these questions will undoubtedly raise further queries about the feminine and masculine symbolism of color itself. Because race and gender can only be understood together, it follows that there must be a gender component to colorism itself. Light skin, in addition to being high status, is also regarded as more feminine, refined, or delicate. Light-skinned women are viewed as extremely feminine and light-skinned men are often feminized as pretty-boys or sissies. Conversely, dark skin is associated with masculinity and dark-skinned men are often considered more virile, dangerous, sexy, and strong. Several of the women I spoke with expressed similar views.

Most of the people I know would gravitate toward the Tysons or the Denzels,[24] the darker-skinned...When you think about it, everybody says they want someone who is tall, dark, and hand-some. They look like they're strong and they're going to protect you.

It seems like darker men are more masculine, like more manly and sexy. They're more protective, especially in the movies, like in *Waiting to Exhale*. And then it seems like the lighter guys, the pretty boys, are talked about as like…gay. The light guys are frail. It's weird.

If dark skin is associated with virility and strength, then can dark skin be a positive for men of color? Perhaps, as more dark-skinned black and Latino male models grace the advertisements people see everyday, dark skin color may become somewhat positive—but not without a cost. Part of the symbolic meaning of dark skin as sexual and strong comes directly from more negative images of men of color as violent rapists or sexually insatiable lovers. The fine line separating positive imagery from negative is a slippery slope. It is yet to be seen if the increasing exposure of dark-skinned models will represent a change in color ideologies or a throwback to the images of the Mandingo and the Latin Lover.

## GLOBALIZATION AND THE NEW RACISM

Globalization, multinational media conglomerates, and the new re-structured world economy all work together to maintain U.S. cultural, economic, and political imperialism. Part of this structure of domina-tion is the exportation of cultural images, arguably all racial in one way or another. The United States exports images of the good life, of white beauty, white affluence, white heroes, and brown and black entertain-ers/criminals.[25] As many people in other countries yearn for the good life offered in the United States, they also yearn for the aesthetic of the United States: light skin, blonde hair, and Anglo facial features. American cultural imperialism explains why women in Korea, surrounded by other Koreans, pay high sums of money to have eyelid surgery to Westernize their eyes. American cultural imperialism explains why women in Saudi Arabia, Tanzania, and Brazil are using toxic skin bleaching creams to try and achieve lighter complexions. American cultural imperialism explains why one of the most common high school graduation presents among the elite in Mexico City is nose surgery. Although these choices may sound extreme, they are all actually quite rational in a context of global racism and U.S. dominance. Unfortunately new eyelids, lighter skin, and new noses are likely to offer their owners better opportunities in a global marketplace. The new global racism transcends national borders and infiltrates cultures and families all over the world. Critical pedagogist Zeus Leonardo argues that under global racism, "Whiteness stamps its claims to superiority, both morally and aesthetically speaking, on its infantilized Other...."[26] Images associated with white America are highly valued and emulated in the global marketplace. This is part of what makes colorism and racism so hard to battle: The images supporting these systems are everywhere and the rewards for whiteness are real.

How can we stop this juggernaut of global racism? Maybe the world is in need of another Black is Beautiful/Brown Pride movement where women are celebrated as Nubian Princesses and Aztec Goddesses...or maybe not. The 1960s movements did much for people of color including instilling pride in their bodies and skin colors. But, replacing one beauty regime with another is not necessarily the way to solve the problem.

> The establishment of an Afrocentric beauty standard was a limited and problematic goal. It was limited because changing the definition of beauty would do little to restructure institutional racism. It was problematic because even a redefinition of beauty reinforced the exaggerated importance of beauty for women, upsetting the racial order, while validating gender hierarchies.[27]

Sociologist Maxine Leeds' assertion is directly on point. It is not adequate to simply invert the standard of beauty, making the darkest beautiful and the lightest ugly. The fact that there are standards at all is objectifying for women. Besides that, altering the beauty standards is a far cry from breaking the clutch of institutional racism in the United States. Instead, we need to change the way we think about beauty, race, and status altogether.

In today's multicultural, transnational, advanced capitalist, highly technological society, how should beauty look? I want to suggest that instead of looking for a new beauty standard, or doing away with the concept of beauty altogether, we might consider that beauty provides a space, both real and imagined, for dialogue and debate. Who is beautiful, the role of race and color in beauty, the meaning of gender and beauty are all questions that provide an opportunity for further discussion on racism, sexism, and justice. By uncovering the beauty queue and debating the high status of white beauty, we expose white racism and female objectification. All of this dialogue happens within the context of the beauty debate.

This is not to suggest that dialogue is all society needs to solve the problem of racial and gender oppression. Individual and collective resistance must also happen. Everyday resistance can occur on many levels. Johnetta Cole and Beverly Guy-Sheftall, in their book *Gender Talk: The Struggle for Women's Equality in African American Communities*, suggest that men and women can criticize and boycott music and music videos that demean women as sexual objects or victims of violence.[28] I suggest the same thing for popular culture images such as magazines, movies, television shows, and music videos that feature only light-skinned women as beautiful, or that demean dark-skinned people. Mexican Americans and African Americans can begin to eliminate value-laden language about skin color in their vocabularies. This will be a significant challenge given how entrenched color and status are in these cultures. People of color also need new image-makers, with innovative ideas about racial representation. More diverse representations of skin tone and status can also lead to a change in attitudes. Lastly, more legal challenges to colorism, such as those described in chapter 1, can help make the penalty for colorism harder to bear. All of these strategies and more will fuel the movement for change.

As Patricia Hill Collins writes in her book *Fighting Words: Black Women and the Search for Justice*, the power of words and self-naming cannot be underestimated.[29] It is essential that African American and Mexican American women begin the process of renaming their beautiful characteristics, not as eye color and hair color, but as pride, intelligence, perseverance, and solidarity with one another. Women of color share many similar experiences of colorism and can learn from their points of difference. If beauty provides a space for dialogue, then let the debates begin, and let the social change quickly follow.

# APPENDIX

## Interview Participants by Race and Skin Color[1]

| First Name | Racial/Ethnic Identity | Skin Color Category |
| --- | --- | --- |
| Belinda | African American | dark |
| Desiree | African American | dark |
| Kitara | African American | dark |
| Marsha | African American | dark |
| Pamela | African American | dark |
| Delilah | African American | medium |
| Jocelyn | African American | medium |
| Maya | African American | medium |
| Rochelle | African American | medium |
| Aisha | African American | light |
| Jackie | African American | light |
| Joyce | African American | light |
| Karla | African American | light |
| Regina | African American | light |
| Simone | African American | light |
| Tisha | African American | light |
| Alicia | Mexican American | dark |
| Isabel | Mexican American | dark |
| Evelyn | Mexican American | medium |
| Barbara | Mexican American | light |
| Catalina | Mexican American | light |
| Diana | Mexican American | light |
| Elena | Mexican American | light |
| Jennifer | Mexican American | light |
| Linda | Mexican American | light |
| Marisel | Mexican American | light |

[1]All names have been changed to maintain the anonymity of the participants.

# NOTES

## Notes to Chapter 1

1. In this book the terms African American and black will be used interchangeably.
2. In this book the terms Mexican American and Chicano or Chicana will be used interchangeably. The term Latino is used specifically to refer to the collective identity of people from Latin America including Puerto Ricans, Central Americans, Cubans, etc., who now reside in the United States. including Puerto Ricans, Central Americans, Cubans, etc.
3. Kathy Russell, Midge Wilson, and Ronald Hall, *The Color Complex: The Politics of Skin Color Among African Americans* (New York: Anchor Books, 1992).
4. Margaret Hunter, "Colorstruck: Skin Color Stratification in the Lives of African American Women," *Sociological Inquiry* 68, no. 4 (1998): 517–35.
5. Marjorie Valbrun, "EEOC Sees Rise in Intrarace Complaints of Color Bias," *Wall Street Journal*, August 7, 2003.
6. Valbrun.
7. Valbrun.
8. Carlos Arce, Edward Murguia, and W. Parker Frisbie, "Phenotype and Life Chances Among Chicanos," *Hispanic Journal of Behavioral Sciences* 9 (1987): 19–32. Michael Hughes and Bradley Hertel, "The Significance of Color Remains: A Study of Life Chances, Mate Selection, and Ethnic Consciousness Among Black Americans," *Social Forces* 68, no. 4 (1990): 1105–20. Verna Keith and Cedric Herring, "Skin Tone and Stratification in the Black Community," *American Journal of Sociology* 97, no. 3 (1991). Richard Seltzer and Robert C. Smith, "Color Differences in the Afro-American Community and the Differences They Make," *Journal of Black Studies* 21, no. 3 (1991): 279–286. Kendrick Brown, "Consequences of Skin Tone Bias for African Americans: Resource Attainment and Psychological and Social Functioning," *African American Research Perspectives* 4 (1998): 55–60. E. Codina and F. Montalvo, "Chicano Phenotype and Depression," *Hispanic Journal of Behavioral Sciences* 16 (1994): 296–306. F. Montalvo *Skin Color and Latinos: The Origins and Contemporary Patterns of Ethnoracial Ambiguity Among Mexican Americans and Puerto Ricans* (monograph) (San Antonio, TX: Our Lady of the Lake University, 1987). Edward Murguia and Edward Telles, "Phenotype and Schooling among Mexican Americans," *Sociology of Education* 69 (1996): 276–89. H.E. Ransford, "Skin Color, Life Chances, and Anti-White Attitude," *Social Problems* 18 (1970): 164–78. J. Relethford, P. Stern, S. P. Catskill, and H.P. Hazuda, "Social Class, Admixture, and Skin Color Variation in Mexican Americans and Anglo Americans Living in San Antonio, Texas," *American Journal of Physical*

*Anthropology* 61 (1983): 97–102. Edward Telles and Edward Murguia, "Phenotypic Discrimination and Income Differences among Mexican Americans," *Social Science Quarterly* 71, no. 4 (1990): 682–96.

9.  Toni Morrison, *Playing in the Dark: Whiteness and the Literary Imagination* (New York: Vintage Books, 1992).

10. St. Clair Drake, *Black Folk Here and There*, Vol. 1. (Los Angeles, UCLA Center for African American Studies: University of California Press, 1987), 23.

11. Ronald Hall, "The Bleaching Syndrome: African Americans' Response to Cultural Domination Vis-à-vis Skin Color," *Journal of Black Studies* 26, no. 2 (1995): 172–84.

12. S. Allen Counter, "Whitening Skin can be Deadly," *Boston Globe*, December 16, 2003.

13. Vicki Ruiz, *From Out of the Shadows: Mexican Women in Twentieth Century America* (New York: Oxford University Press, 1998), 55–56.

14. Maxine Leeds, "Young African-American Women and the Language of Beauty," in *Ideals of Feminine Beauty: Philosophical, Social, and Cultural Dimensions*, ed. Karen Callaghan (London: Greenwood Press, 1994), 6.

15. See also Selena Bond and Thomas Cash, "Black Beauty: Skin Color and Body Images Among African American College-Age Women," *Journal of Applied Social Psychology* 22 (1992): 874–88.

16. Mark E. Hill, "Skin Color and the Perception of Attractiveness Among African Americans: Does Gender Make a Difference?" *Social Psychology Quarterly* 65, no. 1 (2002): 77–91.

17. I use the term social capital here to describe a combination of Pierre Bourdieu's social and symbolic capital. See Pierre Bourdieu, *Distinction* (Cambridge, MA: Harvard University Press, 1984).

18. Richard J. Herrnstein and Charles Murray, *The Bell Curve: Intelligence and Class Structure in American Life* (New York: The Free Press, 1994).

19. St. Clair Drake, *Black Folk Here and There*, Vol. 1.

20. Mary Margaret Fonow and Judith A. Cook, "Back to the Future: A Look at the Second Wave of Feminist Epistemology and Methodology" in *Beyond Methodology: Feminist Scholarship as Lived Research,* eds. Mary Margaret Fonow and Judith A. Cook (Bloomington: Indiana University Press, 1991), 3.

21. Michael Omi and Howard Winant, *Racial Formation in the United States: From the 1960s to the 1990s,* 2nd ed. (New York: Routledge, 1994), 55–56.

22. Virginia R. Dominquez, 1986. *White By Definition: Social Classification in Creole Louisiana* (New Brunswick: Rutgers University Press, 1986).

23. The Rule of Hypodescent is also known as the "one-drop rule."

24. Tomás Almaguer, *Racial Fault Lines: The Historical Origins of White Supremacy in California* (Berkeley: University of California Press, 1994). George Martinez, "Mexican Americans and Whiteness" in *Critical White Studies: Looking Behind the Mirror,* eds. Richard Delgado and Jean Stefancic (Philadelphia: Temple University Press, 1997).

25. Dorothy Smith, "Women's Perspective as Radical Critique of Sociology" in *Feminism and Methodology,* ed. Sandra Harding (Bloomington: Indiana University Press, 1987), Sandra Harding, *Whose Science? Whose Knowledge? Thinking From Women's Lives* (Ithaca, NY: Cornell University Press, 1991). Patricia Hill Collins, "Learning From the Outsider Within: The Sociological Significance of Black Feminist Thought" in *Beyond Methodology: Feminist Scholarship as Lived Research,* eds. Mary Margaret Fonow and Judith A. Cook (Bloomington: Indiana University Press, 1991).

26. Dorothy Smith, "Women's Perspective as Radical Critique of Sociology," 84–85.

27. Deborah King, "Multiple Jeopardy, Multiple Consciousness: The Context of a Black Feminist Ideology," *Signs* 14, no. 1 (1988): 42–72. Maxine Baca Zinn and Bonnie Thornton Dill, "Theorizing Difference from Multiracial Feminism," *Feminist Studies* 22, no. 2 (1996): 321–31.

28. bell hooks, *Ain't I a Woman?* (Boston: South End Press, 1981).

29. For early work in this area see Anna Julia Cooper, *A Voice From the South* (New York: Negro Universities Press, 1892).

30. Deborah King, "Multiple Jeopardy, Multiple Consciousness," 45.

31. Mary Waters, *Ethnic Options: Choosing Identities in America* (Berkeley: University of California Press, 1990).

32. *National Survey of Black Americans, 1979–80*, University of Michigan, James Jackson, Principal Investigator. *National Chicano Survey, 1979–80*, University of Michigan, Carlos Arce, Principal Investigator.

## *Notes to Chapter 2*

1. Dorothy Roberts, *Killing the Black Body* (New York: Pantheon Books, 1997), 23.

2. Joel Williamson, *New People: Miscegenation and Mulattos in the United States* (Baton Rouge: Louisiana University Press, 1995).

3. F. James Davis, *Who Is Black? One Nation's Definition* (University Park: Pennsylvania State University Press, 1991), 5.

4. Allison Davis, *Deep South: A Social Anthropological Study of Caste and Class* (Chicago: University of Chicago Press, 1941).

5. Andrew Billingsley, *Black Families in White America* (Englewood Cliffs, NJ: Prentice Hall, 1968).

6. The enslaved Africans already comprised a continuum of skin colors because of the diversity and mixture among various African groups who were enslaved. The history of sexual violence added to that diversity and created a significant number of very light-skinned, mixed-race people who were identified as African American.

7. E. Franklin Frazier, *The Negro Family in the United States* (New York: The Dryden Press, 1951). Brenda Stevenson, *Life in Black and White: Family and Community in the Slave South* (New York: Oxford University Press, 1996).

8. Bettye Collier-Thomas and James Turner, "Race, Class, and Color: The African American Discourse on Identity," *Journal of American Ethnic History* 14 (1994): 5–32.

9. Frazier, *The Negro Family in the United States*, 19.

10. Willard B. Gatewood, *Aristocrats of Color: The Black Elite 1880–1920* (Bloomington: Indiana University Press, 1990).

11. Elizabeth Mullins and Paul Sites, "The Origins of Contemporary Eminent Black Americans: A Three Generation Analysis of Social Origin," *American Sociological Review* 49 (1984): 672–85.

12. G. F. Edwards, *The Negro Professional Class* (Glencoe, IL: The Free Press, 1959). E. Franklin Frazier, *Black Bourgeoisie* (New York: Collier Books, 1957).

13. E. B. Reuter, *The Mulatto in the United States* (New York: Negro University Press, 1918).

14. Thomas F. Gossett, *Race: The History of an Idea in America* (Dallas: Southern Methodist University Press, 1963).

15. The attribution of goodness and evil to whiteness and blackness, respectively, dates back to the 1400s with the earliest European colonial actions. For a fuller discussion of this topic in the period 1550–1812, see Winthrop Jordan, *White Over Black* (Chapel Hill: University of North Carolina Press, 1968). However, for the purposes of this book, I focus my discussion of these racist ideologies on the 1800s in the United States.

16. J. Blaine Hudson, "The African Diaspora and the 'Black Atlantic': An African American Perspective," *Negro History Bulletin* 6, no. 4 (1997), 11.

17. Omi and Winant, 53–76.

18. Albert Memmi, *The Colonizer and the Colonized* (Boston: Beacon Press, 1965). Klaus Ernst, "Racialism, Racialist Ideology, and Colonialism, Past and Present," in *Sociological Theories: Race and Colonialism* (United Kingdom: UNESCO, 1980). Frantz Fanon, *Black Skin White Masks* (New York: Grove Weidenfeld, 1967).

19. Drake, 17.
20. Bernal Díaz del Castillo, *The Conquest of New Spain* (Baltimore: Penguin Books, 1963).
21. Rodolfo Acuña, *Occupied America* (New York: Harper and Row, 1988).
22. Magnus Mörner, *Race Mixture in the History of Latin America* (Boston: Little, Brown, 1967).
23. Irene Blea, *La Chicana and the Intersection of Race, Class, and Gender* (Westport, CT: Praeger, 1992), 43.
24. Antonia Castañeda, "Sexual Violence in the Politics of and Policies of Conquest: Amerindian Women and the Spanish Conquest of Alta California," in *Building With Our Hands: New Directions in Chicana Studies,* eds. Adela de la Torre and Beatríz M. Pesquera (Berkeley: University of California Press, 1993), 29.
25. Los Angeles County Museum of Art, *Inventing Race: Casta Painting and Eighteenth-Century Mexico;* (Los Angeles: LACMA, 2004).
26. José Vasconcelos, *La Raza Cósmica, Misión de la Raza Iberoamericana* (Paris: Agencia Mundial de Librería, 1925).
27. Andrés Guerrero, *A Chicano Theology* (New York: Orbis Books, 1987), 123.
28. Almaguer, 32.
29. Almaguer, 8.
30. Mario Barrera, *Race and Class in the Southwest* (Notre Dame: University of Notre Dame Press, 1979).
31. G. Martinez, 212.
32. Vilma Ortiz, "The Mexican-Origin Population: Permanent Working Class or Emerging Middle Class?," in *Ethnic Los Angeles,* eds. Roger Waldinger and Mehdi Bozorgmehr (New York: Russell Sage, 1996).
33. Chris Kraul, "Illegal Immigrants Receive a One-Way Ticket to Mexico" *Los Angeles Times,* July 13, 2004, part A, page 1.
34. Sandra Harding, *Feminism and Methodology* (Bloomington: Indiana University Press, 1987), 84.
35. Patricia Hill Collins, *Black Feminist Thought* (New York: Routledge, 1991), 26.
36. Rita Freedman, *Beauty Bound* (Lexington, MA: Lexington Books, 1986), 6.
37. Bourdieu uses the term social capital to refer to things that are not obviously of worth, but may be transformed into or traded for economic capital.
38. Naomi Wolf, *The Beauty Myth: How Images of Beauty are Used Against Women* (New York: Doubleday, 1991).
39. Wolf, 21.
40. Cheryl Harris, "Whiteness as Property," in *Critical Race Theory,* eds. Kimberlé Crenshaw, Neil Gotanda, Gary Peller, and Kendall Thomas (New York: The New Press, 1995).
41. Harris, 277.
42. St. Clair Drake and Horace R. Cayton, *Black Metropolis* (New York: Harcourt Brace, 1945), 498.
43. Collins, *Black Feminist Thought,* 88.
44. Lois Banner, *American Beauty* (New York: Knopf, 1983).
45. Richard Udry, Karl Baumann, and Charles Chase, "Skin Color, Status, and Mate Selection," *American Journal of Sociology* 76, no. 4 (1971): 722.
46. Udry, Baumann, and Chase.
47. Robin Lakoff and Racquel Scherr, *Face Value: The Politics of Beauty* (New York: Routledge, 1984), 258.
48. Drake and Cayton.
49. Ruiz, 57.
50. Ruiz, 57.

51. Joane Nagel, *Race, Ethnicity, and Sexuality: Intimate Intersections and Forbidden Frontiers* (New York: Oxford University Press, 2003).

52. Paula Giddings, *When and Where I Enter* (New York: Quill William Morrow, 1984). K. Sue Jewell, *From Mammy to Miss America and Beyond: Cultural Images and the Shaping of U.S. Social Policy* (New York: Routledge, 1993).

53. Castañeda

54. Emma Pérez, "Speaking from the Margin: Uninvited Discourse on Sexuality and Power," in *Building With Our Hands: New Directions in Chicana Studies,* eds. Adela de la Torre and Beatríz Pesquera (Berkeley: University of California Press, 1993).

55. Jenny Rivera, "Domestic Violence Against Latinas by Latino Males: An Analysis of Race, National Origin, and Gender Differentials," in *Critical Race Feminism,* ed. Adrien Katherine Wing (New York: New York University Press, 1997).

56. Almaguer, 61.

57. Carlos E. Cortés, "Chicanas in Film: History of an Image," in *Latin Looks: Images of Latinas and Latinos in the U.S. Media,* ed. Clara E. Rodriguez (Boulder, Colorado: Westview Press, 1997), 128.

58. Rivera, 260.

59. Leith Mullings, "Images, Ideology, and Women of Color," in *Women of Color in U.S. Society,* eds. Maxine Baca Zinn and Bonnie Thornton Dill (Philadelphia: Temple University Press, 1994).

60. hooks, 24.

61. Cedric Herring, "Skin Deep: Race and Complexion in the Color-Blind Era," in *Skin/Deep: How Race and Complexion Matter in the Color-Blind Era,* eds. Cedric Herring, Verna M. Keith, Hayward Derrick Horton (Urbana: University of Illinois Press, 2004), 7.

62. National Association for the Advancement of Colored People, *Thirty Years of Lynching in the U.S. 1889–1918* (New York: Negro Universities Press, 1969).

63. George Fredrickson, *White Supremacy* (Oxford: Oxford University Press, 1981).

64. Walter Howard, *Lynchings: Extralegal Violence in Florida During the 1930s* (London: Associated Universities Press, 1995), 20.

65. Angela Davis, *Women, Race, and Class* (New York: Vintage Books, 1981), 184.

66. Paul Hoch, *White Hero Black Beast: Racism, Sexism and the Mask of Masculinity* (London: Pluto Press, 1979).

67. Mullings, 284.

68. Calvin Hernton, *Sex and Racism in America* (New York: Grove Press, 1965), 19.

69. Almaguer, 62.

70. Joan Moore and Harry Pachon, *Hispanics in the United States* (Englewood Cliffs, NJ: Prentice Hall, 1985).

71. hooks, *Ain't I a Woman.*

72. Bonnie Thorton Dill, "The Dialectics of Black Womanhood," in *Black Women in America,* eds. Micheline Malson, Elisabeth Mudimbe-Boyi, Jean O'Barr, and Mary Wyer (Chicago: University of Chicago Press, 1988), 65.

73. Maxine Baca Zinn, "Gender and Ethnic Identity Among Chicanos," *Frontiers* 5, no. 2 (1980): 18–24.

74. Miguel Montiel, "The Social Science Myth of the Mexican American Family," *El Grito* 3 (1970): 56–63.

75. Denise Segura and Beatriz M. Pesquera, "Beyond Indifference and Antipathy: The Chicana Movement and Chicana Feminist Discourse," *Aztlan* 19, no. 2 (1988): 69–92.

76. Gloria Anzaldúa, *Borderlands: The New Mestiza* (San Francisco: Aunt Lute Books, 1987).

77. Alma Garcia, "The Development of Chicana Feminist Discourse, 1970–1980," *Gender and Society* 3, no. 2 (1989): 223.

78. Cynthia Orozco, "Sexism in Chicano Studies and the Community," in *Chicana Voices: Intersections of Class, Race, and Gender,* eds. Teresa Córdova, Norma Cantú, Gilberto Cardenas, Juan García, and Christine Sierra (Albuquerque: University of New Mexico Press, 1990).

79. Clayborne Carson, *In Struggle: SNCC and the Black Awakening of the 1960s* (Cambridge: Harvard University Press, 1981).

## Notes to Chapter 3

1. A different version of this chapter was previously published. Margaret Hunter, "'If You're Light, You're Alright': Light Skin Color as Social Capital for Women of Color," *Gender & Society* 16, no. 2 (2002): 175–93.

2. Dorothy Holland and Margaret Eisenhart, *Educated in Romance* (Chicago: University of Chicago Press, 1990).

3. Lynne Luciano, *Looking Good: Male Body Image in Modern America* (New York: Hill and Wang, 2001).

4. Patricia Zavella, "Reflections on Diversity Among Chicanas," in *Challenging Fronteras: Structuring Latina and Latino Lives in the U.S.,* eds. Mary Romero, Pierrette Hondagneu-Sotelo, and Vilma Ortiz (New York: Routledge, 1997).

5. Margo Okazawa-Rey, Tracy Robinson, and Janie V. Ward, "Black Women and the Politics of Skin Color and Hair," *Women's Studies Quarterly* 14, nos. 1,2 (1986).

6. Collins, *Black Feminist Thought.*

7. Cherríe Moraga, "La Güera," in *This Bridge Called My Back: Radical Writings by Women of Color,* eds. Gloria Anzaldúa and Cherríe Moraga (New York: Kitchen Table Press, 1983).

8. These statistics for educational attainment deviate somewhat from the national average. Nationally, 36 percent of Mexican American women graduated from high school only and 52 percent of African American women graduated from high school only in 1980 (see Vilma Ortiz, "Women of Color: A Demographic Overview, in *Women of Color in U.S. Society,* eds. Maxine Baca Zinn and Bonnie Thornton Dill (Philadelphia: Temple University Press, 1994).

9. For both of these variables there were a large number of missing cases because many people did not know this information. In order to retain several hundred cases in the analysis, respondents with unknown parental education were assigned the median number of years of education for the known cases.

10. There are systematic differences between those who know their parents' education and those who do not. Respondents were more likely to know their parents' education levels if they were higher rather than lower. In order to account for this difference, two other variables were created: don't know mother's education and don't know father's education, to account for any difference between those respondents who knew their parents' levels of education and those who did not. These are dummy variables using those who did not know their parents' education as the baseline category (see Claude Fischer, Michael Hout, Martín S. Jankowski, Samuel Lucas, Ann Swidler, and Kim Voss, *Inequality by Design: Cracking the Bell Curve Myth* (Princeton, NJ: Princeton University Press, 1996).

11. There are other possible explanations of why one may not know her mother's education. It is possible that the respondent did not grow up with their mother, or that his or her mother died at a young age. However, it most likely that people are less likely to know their mother's level of education if it is low than if it is high.

12. Max Haller, "Marriage, Women, and Social Stratification: A Theoretical Critique," *American Journal of Sociology* 86, no. 4 (1981): 766–95. Murray Webster, Jr. and James Driskell Jr., "Beauty As Status," *American Journal of Sociology* 89, no. 1 (1983): 140–65.

13. Diane K. Lewis, "A Response to Inequality: Black Women, Racism, and Sexism," in *Black Women in America*, eds. Micheline Malson, Elisabeth Mudimbe-Boyi, Jean F. O'Barr, and Mary Wyer (Chicago: University of Chicago Press, 1988).

14. Arnoldo De León, *They Called Them Greasers: Anglo Attitudes Toward Mexicans in Texas, 1821–1900* (Austin: University of Texas Press, 1983). Guillermo Lux and Maurilio Vigil, "Return to Aztlán: The Chicano Rediscovers His Indian Past," in *Aztlán: Essays on the Chicano Homeland*, eds. Rudolfo Anaya and Francisco Lomelí (Albuquerque: University of New Mexico Press, 1989).

15. Maxine S. Thompson and Verna Keith, "The Blacker the Berry: Gender, Skin Tone, Self-Esteem, and Self-Efficacy," *Gender & Society* 15, no. 3 (2001): 336–57.

16. Many articles appearing in popular magazines such as Ebony, Jet, and Essence have covered the issue of colorism in the African American community. Toni Morrison deals with the issue of color and self-hate in her book, *The Bluest Eye*, and Spike Lee takes up the issue in his film, *School Daze*.

## Notes to Chapter 4

1. Paraphrase of an interview segment with Kitara, an African American interview participant.

2. Arce, Murguia, and Frisbie.

3. Diane Taylor, "Stitched Up: Where Plastic Surgeons Profit From Teenage Dreams," *The Mirror*, December 7, 2002.

4. Virginia Blum, *Flesh Wounds: The Culture of Cosmetic Surgery* (Berkeley: University of California Press, 2003), 2–10.

5. Many people with darker skin tones experience raised, dark scars after surgery, called keloids. This was a significant deterrent to elective surgery for many people of color. Improved technologies in the cosmetic surgery industry have greatly reduced the chances of keloid scarring.

6. Cosmetic procedures is a more general term that includes cosmetic surgeries, such as breast augmentations, or nose jobs, but that also includes non-surgical cosmetic procedures such as chemical peels, BOTOX injections, and laser hair removal.

7. American Society for Aesthetic Plastic Surgery, "2002 Report," http://www.surgery.org.

8. American Society for Aesthetic Plastic Surgery, "2002 Report," http://www.surgery.org.

9. American Academy of Facial Plastic and Reconstructive Surgeons, http://www.aafprs.org.

10. Kathy Davis, *Reshaping the Female Body* (New York: Routledge, 1995).

11. American Society of Aesthetic Plastic Surgeons, "2002 Statistics," http://www.cosmeticplasticsurgerystatistics.com/statistics.html.

12. American Society for Aesthetic Plastic Surgery, "2002 Report," http://www.surgery.org..

13. Elizabeth Haiken, *Venus Envy: A History of Cosmetic Surgery* (Baltimore: Johns Hopkins University Press, 1997), 175–227.

14. American Academy of Facial Plastic and Reconstructive Surgeons, http://www.facial-plastic-surgery.org/media/stats_polls/m_stats.html.

15. Kathryn Pauly Morgan, "Women and the Knife: Cosmetic Surgery and the Colonization of Women's Bodies," in *The Politics of Women's Bodies: Sexuality, Appearance, and Behavior*, ed. Rose Weitz (New York: Oxford University Press, 1998).

16. Morgan, 155.

17. Fred Guterl and Michael Hastings, with Sudip Mazumdar, Sarah Schafer, B. J. Lee, and Sonia Kolesnikov-Jessop, "The Global Makeover," *Newsweek*, November 10, 2003.

18. Guterl et al., 48.
19. Guterl et al., 48.
20. American Society of Plastic Surgeons, "Plastic Surgery Helps African Americans and Other Ethnic Populations Achieve Individual Standards of Beauty," *Plastic Surgery Today* (February 2002), http://www.plasticsurgery.org.
21. American Academy of Facial Plastic and Reconstructive Surgeons, "Facial Plastic Surgery Enhances Ethnic Features," *Facial Plastic Surgery Today* 10, no. 3 (1996), http://www.facial-plastic-surgery.org/patient/fps_today/vol10_3/vol10_3pg1.html.
22. American Academy of Facial Plastic and Reconstructive Surgeons, *Facial Plastic Surgery Today* (May 2002,) http://www.prnewswire.co.uk/cgi/news/release?id=84796.
23. The American Society for Aesthetic Plastic Surgery, "2001 ASAPS Statistics: Trends — Ethnic Diversity,"http://surgery.org/press/news-stats-14.asp.
24. Eugenia Kaw, "Medicalization of Racial Features: Asian American Women and Cosmetic Surgery," in *The Politics of Women's Bodies: Sexuality, Appearance, and Behavior,* ed. Rose Weitz (New York: Oxford University Press, 1998), 175.
25. Steven M. Hoefflin, *Ethnic Rhinoplasty* (New York: Springer-Verlag, 1998), xv, 2, 3.
26. Oscar M. Ramírez, "Facial Plastic Surgery in the Hispano-American Patient," in *Ethnic Considerations in Facial Aesthetic Surgery,* ed. W. Earle Matory Jr. (Philadelphia: Lippincott-Raven, 1998), 310–11.
27. Hoefflin, 2.
28. Ramírez, 310.
29. Maxine Leeds Craig, *Ain't I a Beauty Queen: Black Women, Beauty, and the Politics of Race* (New York: Oxford University Press, 2002), 40–41. Also see Tracy L. Robinson and Janie V. Ward, "African American Adolescents and Skin Color," *Journal of Black Psychology* 21, no. 3 (1995): 256–74. Stephanie Irby Coard, Alfiee M. Breland, and Patricia Raskin, "Perceptions of and Preferences for Skin Color, Black Racial Identity, and Self-Esteem Among African Americans," *Journal of Applied Social Psychology* 31, no. 11 (2001): 2256–74.
30. Craig, 41.
31. Sara Goering, "Conformity Through Cosmetic Surgery: The Medical Erasure of Race and Disability," in *Science and Other Cultures: Issues in Philosophies of Science and Technology* (New York: Routledge, 2003), 175.
32. American Academy of Facial Plastic and Reconstructive Surgeons, "Facial Plastic Surgery Enhances Ethnic Features," *Facial Plastic Surgery Today* 10, no. 3 (1996), http://www.facial-plastic-surgery.org/patient/fps_today/vol10_3/vol10_3pg1.html.
33. Suzanne Fraser, *Cosmetic Surgery, Gender, and Culture* (New York: Palgrave Macmillan, 2003), 95.
34. Jan R. Adams, *Everything Women of Color Should Know About Cosmetic Surgery* (New York: St. Martin's Press, 2000), 3–4.
35. Adams, 4.
36. Nancy Etcoff, *Survival of the Prettiest: The Science of Beauty* (New York: Anchor Books, 2000).
37. Adams, 4.
38. While it is true that African Americans and Latinos appear more frequently in all media forms than they have in the past, many other people of color still have limited roles including Asian Americans, Native Americans, and Arab Americans.
39. Arlene M. Davila, *Latinos, Inc.* (Berkeley: University of California Press, 2001).
40. Deborah A. Sullivan, *Cosmetic Surgery: The Cutting Edge of Commercial Medicine in America* (New Brunswick: Rutgers University Press, 2001), 5–6.
41. Audre Lorde, *Sister Outsider* (New York: Crossing Press, 1984).

## Notes to Chapter 5

1. Quote from an interview with Pearl Marsh in Maxine Leeds Craig, *Ain't I A Beauty Queen?*
2. Freedman, *Beauty Bound,* 1.
3. Glen Elder, "Appearance and Education in Marriage Mobility," *American Sociological Review* 34 (1969): 519–33. Elaine Hatfield and Susan Sprecher, *Mirror, Mirror: The Importance of Looks in Everyday Life* (Albany: State University of New York Press, 1986). Webster and Driskell, "Beauty as Status."
4. Chapters five and six are based on data from twenty-six qualitative interviews with African American and Mexican American women. The interviews all took place in 1998 on the campus of a large, West Coast university. Students in several large classes were asked if they would like to participate in a study on skin tone. This method yielded interviews with sixteen African American women and ten Mexican American women of various skin colors (see Appendix A). As other studies of colorism have, I used a color palette as a method of assessing lightness or darkness. For each participant, lightness and darkness were assessed in relation to the members of her own ethnic group. This meant that the light-skinned African Americans were generally darker than the light-skinned Mexican Americans.
5. My interview style was influenced by the feminist research methodology literature. See Marjorie DeVault, "Talking and Listening from Women's Standpoint: Feminist Strategies for Interviewing and Analysis," *Social Problems* 37, no. 1 (1990): 96–116. Mary Margaret Fonow and Judith A. Cook, eds., Beyond Methodology: Feminist Scholarship as Lived Research (Bloomington: Indiana University Press, 1991). Maria Mies, "Towards a Methodology for Feminist Research" in *Theories of Women's Studies,* eds. G. Bowles and R. Klein (New York: Routledge, 1983). Liz Stanley and Sue Wise, *Breaking Out: Feminist Consciousness and Feminist Research* (New York: Routledge, 1983). Catherine Kohler Riessman, "When Gender is Not Enough: Women Interviewing Women," *Gender and Society,* 1, no. 2 (1987): 172–207. Ann Oakley, "Interviewing Women: A Contradiction in Terms" in *Doing Feminist Research,* ed. Helen Roberts (New York: Routledge, 1981). Feminist research methods that focus on interaction and liberation have been developed in response to more traditional, and often male-centered, research methods. Oakley argues that feminist interviewing need not be limited to asked and answered questions, but should include a more interactive dialogue. Not only does this create a more personable and inter-subjective experience for the interviewer and interviewee, but it also yields better, or even more accurate data. Treating the participant as an expert on her own experiences with valuable insights to share also reduces the objectification of the participant and constructs an interview setting that can be, at least ideally, transformative and liberating for both the interviewer and the interviewee.
6. M. Belinda Tucker and Claudia Mitchell-Kernan, "Psychological Well-Being and Perceived Marital Opportunity Among Single African American, Latina, and White Women," *Journal of Comparative Family Studies* 29, no. 1 (1998): 57–72.
7. Patricia Hill Collins, *Black Feminist Thought,* 81.
8. Ayana D. Byrd and Lori L. Tharps, *Hair Story: Untangling the Roots of Black Hair in America* (New York: St. Martin's Griffin, 2001).
9. Noliwe M. Rooks, *Hair Raising: Beauty, Culture, and African American Women* (New Brunswick: Rutgers University Press, 1996). See also Kia Lilly Caldwell, "Look at Her Hair": The Body Politics of Black Womanhood in Brazil," *Transforming Anthropology* 11, no. 2 (2003): 18–29.

10. See Carolivia Herron, *Nappy Hair* (New York: Dragonfly Books, 1998). bell hooks, *Happy to Be Nappy* (New York: Hyperion Press, 1999).

11. Michelle Wallace, "Anger in Isolation: A Black Feminist's Search for Sisterhood" in *Words of Fire: An Anthology of African American Feminist Thought*, ed. Beverly Guy-Sheftall (New York: The New Press, 1995), 220.

12. Zavella, "Reflections on Diversity Among Chicanas," 190.

13. Zavella, "Reflections on Diversity Among Chicanas," 190.

14. Anthony J. Cortese, *Provocateur: Images of Women and Minorities in Advertising* (New York: Rowman & Littlefield, 1999), 91–96.

15. Ronald Hall, "Dark Skin and the Cultural Ideal of Masculinity," *Journal of African American Men* 1, no. 3 (1995): 37–62.

16. Patricia Hill Collins, *Black Sexual Politics: African Americans, Gender, and the New Racism* (New York: Routledge, 2004).

17. Margaret Hunter, Walter R. Allen, and Edward E. Telles, "The Significance of Skin Color Among African Americans and Mexican Americans," *African American Research Perspectives* 7, no. 1 (2001).

18. Udry, Baumann, and Chase.

19. Fanon, 63.

20. Obiagele Lake, *Blue Veins and Kinky Hair: Naming and Color Consciousness in African America* (Westport, CT: Praeger, 2003).

## Notes to Chapter 6

1. F. James Davis, 7.

2. Barbara Carrasco, interview by Jeffrey J. Rangel, *Smithsonian Archives of American Art*, April 13, 1999.

3. Maria P. P. Root, "Mixed Race Women," in *Race Sex: Their Sameness, Difference, and Interplay*, ed. Naomi Zack (New York: Routledge, 1997).

4. Vilma Ortiz and Carlos Arce, "Language Orientation and Mental Health Status Among Persons of Mexican Descent," *Hispanic Journal of Behavioral Sciences*, 6 (1984): 127–43. David Lopez, *Language Maintenance and Shift in the U.S. Today: The Basic Patterns and Their Implications* (Los Alamitos, CA: National Center for Bilingual Research, 1982).

5. Howard Freeman, David Armor, Michael Ross, and Thomas Pettigrew, "Color Gradation and Attitudes among Middle Income Negroes," *American Sociological Review* 31 (1966): 365–74. Ozzie Edwards, "Skin Color as a Variable in Racial Attitudes of Black Urbanites" *Journal of Black Studies* 3 (1973): 473–83. H. Edward Ransford, "Skin Color, Life Chances, and Anti-White Attitude," *Social Problems* 18 (1970): 164–78. F. Montalvo, *Skin Color and Latinos: The Origins and Contemporary Patterns of Ethnoracial Ambiguity Among Mexican Americans and Puerto Ricans* (monograph) (San Antonio, TX: Our Lady of the Lake University, 1987). Hughes and Hertel. Ronald Hall, "'The Bleaching Syndrome': Implications of Light Skin for Hispanic American Assimilation," *Hispanic Journal of Behavioral Sciences* 16, no. 3 (1994): 307–14.

6. Alan Knight, "Racism, Revolution, and Indigenismo: Mexico, 1910–1940" in *The Idea of Race in Latin America*, ed. Richard Graham (Austin: University of Texas Press, 1990).

7. Although I use the term Latino throughout the book, Diana routinely used the term "Hispanic," so I use it when paraphrasing her words.

8. Judy Scales-Trent, *Notes of a White Black Woman: Race, Color, and Community* (University Park: Pennsylvania State University Press, 1995), 67–68.

9. Phillip J. Bowman, Ray Muhammad, and Mosi Ifatunji, "Skin Tone, Class, and Racial Attitudes Among African Americans," in *Skin/Deep: How Race and Complexion Matter*

*in the 'Color-Blind' Era,* eds. Cedric Herring, Verna M. Keith, and Hayward Derrick Horton (Urbana: University of Illinois Press, 2004), 128–58.

10. Lawrence Otis Graham, Our Kind of People: Inside America's Black Upper Class (New York: Perennial, 2000).

## *Notes to Chapter 7*

1. Mark Hill, "Color Differences in the Socioeconomic Status of African American Men: Results of a Longitudinal Study," *Social Forces* 78, no. 4 (2000): 1437–60.
2. Rodolfo Espino and Michael Franz, "Latino Phenotypic Discrimination Revisited: The Impact of Skin Color on Occupational Status." *Social Science Quarterly* 83, no. 2 (2002): 612.
3. Darryl Fears, "Race Divides Hispanics, Report Says; Integration and Income Vary With Skin Color," *Washington Post,* July 14, 2003.
4. Richard D. Alba, John R. Logan, and Brian J. Stults, "The Changing Neighborhood Contexts of the Immigrant Metropolis," Social Forces 79, no. 2 (2000): 587–621.
5. Eduardo Bonilla-Silva, "We are all Americans! The Latin Americanization of Racial Stratification in the USA," *Race and Society* 5, no. 1 (2002): 3–17.
6. Amanda Lewis, Mark Chesler, and Tyrone Forman, "The Impact of 'Colorblind' Ideologies on Students of Color: Intergroup Relations at a Predominately White University," *Journal of Negro Education* 69, no. 1–2 (2000): 74–91.
7. Margaret L. Hunter and Kimberly D. Nettles, "What About the White Women?: Racial Politics in a Women's Studies Classroom," *Teaching Sociology* 27 (1999): 385–397.
8. Walter R. Allen, Robert Teranishi, Gniesha Dinwiddie, and Gloria Gonzalez, "Knocking at Freedom's Door: Race, Equity, and Affirmative Action in U.S. Higher Education," *Journal of Negro Education* 69, no. 1–2 (2000): 3–11.
9. The University of Michigan was a defendant in two separate and related cases. They won the Grutter v. Bollinger case about their law school admissions and lost Gratz v. Bollinger about their undergraduate admissions policy. In both cases, however, the right to use race as one deciding factor in university admissions was maintained.
10. Although originally called the Racial Privacy Initiative, the California courts later renamed the initiative Race, Ethnicity, Color or National Origin Classification for clarity.
11. Connerly and his colleagues actually made an exemption for a few things including medical data. However, in terms of public relations, scaring the public about its health turned out to be a more effective strategy for beating this initiative than acknowledging the need to monitor persistent racial discrimination.
12. Beth McMurtrie, "The Quota Quandry," *The Chronicle of Higher Education,* Feb. 13, 2004, sec. A.
13. Vânia Penha-Lopes, "Race South of the Equator: Reexamining the Intersection of Color and Class in Brazil," in *Skin/Deep: How Race and Complexion Matter in the 'Color-Blind' Era,* eds. Cedric Herring, Verna M. Keith, and Hayward Derrick Horton (Urbana: University of Illinois Press, 2004).
14. Angela James, "Making Sense of Race and Racial Classification," *Race and Society* 4, no. 2 (2001): 235–47.
15. MEChA is the student organization Movimiento Estudiantil Chicano de Aztlán.
16. Bonilla-Silva, Eduardo, *"We are all Americans!"* p. 10.
17. Hayward Derrick Horton and Lori Latrice Sykes, "Toward a Critical Demography of Neo-Mulattoes: Structural Change and Diversity Within the Black Population," in *Skin/Deep: How Race and Complexion Matter in the 'Color-Blind' Era,* eds. Cedric Herring, Verna M. Keith, and Hayward Derrick Horton (Urbana: University of Illinois Press, 2004), 167.

18. Interview with the author from set of 26 qualitative interviews.

19. Interview with the author from set of 26 qualitative interviews.

20. Bonilla-Silva, *Eduardo, "We are all Americans!"* p.4.

21. Kerry Ann Rockquemore, "Between Black and White: Exploring the "Biracial" *Experi-ence,"* *Race and Society* 1, no. 2 (1998): 202.

22. Because of limitations in the data, this study did not investigate the dating/marriage market among lesbian women. The National Survey of Black Americans and the Na-tional Chicano Survey only ascertained information on spouses who were "legally" married: that excludes all marriages, legal or otherwise, between two women, as well as co-habitating heterosexual couples who were unmarried.

23. I purposefully used gender-neutral terms when asking about people they had dated in the past and when I asked about what famous people they found attractive I asked about both men and women. Unfortunately, none of this yielded any lesbian, or bisexual, women—at least none that identified themselves in any way to me. I think the problem was in the self-selection of the sample. When I pitched the opportunity to participate in these interviews in front of several large sociology classes, I told them I would ask them about dating. This may have been enough to discourage any lesbian or bisexual women from participating. They may have assumed that I would be asking only about heterosexual dating, or they may have been afraid of a homophobic reaction from me about their dates with women. In the future, I would be more explicit about the fact that lesbian, straight, and bisexual women are encouraged to participate.

24. This refers to the model Tyson Beckford, and the actor Denzel Washington, who are both very handsome, dark-skinned celebrities.

25. I include entertainers and criminals as one category because it seems that most popular culture images show African Americans and Latinos as murderers, drug traffickers, thieves, etc. These images serve as entertainment to the white and nonwhite public.

26. Zeus Leonardo, "The Souls of White Folk: Critical Pedagogy, Whiteness Studies, and Globalization Discourse," *Race Ethnicity, and Education* 5, no. 1 (2002): 29–50.

27. Leeds, 1.

28. Johnetta Cole and Beverly Guy-Sheftall, *Gender Talk: The Struggle for Women's Equality in African American Communities* (New York: Striver's Row. 2003).

29. Patricia Hill Collins, *Fighting Words: Black Women and the Search for Justice* (Min-neapolis: University of Minnesota Press, 1998).

# BIBLIOGRAPHY

Acuña, Rodolfo. *Occupied America*. New York: Harper and Row, 1988.

Adams, Jan R. *Everything Women of Color Should Know About Cosmetic Surgery*. New York: St. Martin's Press, 2000.

Alba, Richard D., John R. Logan, and Brian J. Stults. "The Changing Neighborhood Contexts of the Immigrant Metropolis." *Social Forces* 79, no. 2 (2000): 587–621.

Allen, Walter R., Robert Teranishi, Gniesha Dinwiddie, and Gloria Gonzalez. "Knocking at Freedom's Door: Race, Equity, and Affirmative Action in U.S. Higher Education." *Journal of Negro Education* 69, no. 1–2 (2000): 3–11.

Almaguer, Tomás. *Racial Fault Lines*. Berkeley: University of California Press, 1994.

American Academy of Facial Plastic and Reconstructive Surgeons, http://www.aafprs.org.

———. "Facial Plastic Surgery Enhances Ethnic Features." *Facial Plastic Surgery Today* 10, no. 3 (1996), http://www.facial-plastic-surgery.org/patient/fps_today/vol10_3/vol10_3pg1.html.

———. *Facial Plastic Surgery Today*. (May 2002), http://www.prnewswire.co.uk/cgi/news/release?id=84796.

The American Society for Aesthetic Plastic Surgery. "2002 Report." http://www.surgery.org.

The American Society for Aesthetic Plastic Surgery. "2001 ASAPS Statistics: Trends — Ethnic Diversity." http://surgery.org/press/news-stats-14.asp.

American Society of Plastic Surgeons. "Plastic Surgery Helps African Americans and Other Ethnic Populations Achieve Individual Standards of Beauty." *Plastic Surgery Today* (February 2002), http://www.plasticsurgery.org.

Anzaldúa, Gloria. *Borderlands: The New Mestiza*. San Francisco: Aunt Lute Books, 1987.

Arce, Carlos, Edward Murguia, and W. Parker Frisbie. "Phenotype and Life Chances Among Chicanos." *Hispanic Journal of Behavioral Sciences*, 9 (1987): 19–32.

Banner, Lois. *American Beauty*. New York: Knopf, 1983.

Barrera, Mario. *Race and Class in the Southwest*. Notre Dame, IN: University of Notre Dame Press, 1979.

Billingsley, Andrew. *Black Families in White America*. Englewood Cliffs, NJ: Prentice Hall Inc., 1968.

Blea, Irene. *La Chicana and the Intersection of Race, Class, and Gender*. Westport, CT: Praeger, 1992.

Blum, Virginia. *Flesh Wounds: The Culture of Cosmetic Surgery*. Berkeley: University of California Press, 2003.

Bond, Selena, and Thomas Cash. "Black Beauty: Skin Color and Body Images Among African American College-Age Women." *Journal of Applied Social Psychology* 22 (1992): 874–88.

Bonilla-Silva, Eduardo. "We are all Americans! The Latin Americanization of Racial Stratification in the USA." *Race and Society* 5, no. 1 (2002): 3–17.

Bourdieu, Pierre. *Distinction*. Cambridge: Harvard University Press, 1984.

Bowman, Phillip J., Ray Muhammad, and Mosi Ifatunji. "Skin Tone, Class, and Racial Attitudes Among African Americans." In *Skin/Deep: How Race and Complexion Matter in the 'Color-Blind' Era*, eds. Cedric Herring, Verna M. Keith, and Hayward Derrick Horton. Urbana: University of Illinois Press, 2004, 128–58.

Brown, Kendrick. "Consequences of Skin Tone Bias for African Americans: Resource Attainment and Psychological and Social Functioning." *African American Research Perspectives* 4 (1998): 55–60.

Byrd, Ayana D., and Lori L. Tharps. *Hair Story: Untangling the Roots of Black Hair in America*. New York: St. Martin's Griffin, 2001.

Caldwell, Kia Lilly. "'Look at Her Hair': The Body Politics of Black Womanhood in Brazil." *Transforming Anthropology* 11, no. 2 (2003): 18–29.

Carrasco, Barbara. Interview by Jeffrey J. Rangel. *Smithsonian Archives of American Art*, April 13, 1999.

Carson, Clayborne. *In Struggle: SNCC and the Black Awakening of the 1960s*. Cambridge: Harvard University Press, 1981.

Castañeda, Antonia. "Sexual Violence in the Politics of and Policies of Conquest: Amerindian Women and the Spanish Conquest of Alta California." In *Building With Our Hands: New Directions in Chicana Studies*, eds. Adela de la Torre and Beatríz M. Pesquera. Berkeley: University of California Press, 1993.

Coard, Stephanie Irby, Alfiee M. Breland, and Patricia Raskin. "Perceptions of and Preferences for Skin Color, Black Racial Identity, and Self-Esteem Among African Americans." *Journal of Applied Social Psychology* 31, no. 11 (2001): 2256–74.

Codina, E., and F. Montalvo. "Chicano Phenotype and Depression." *Hispanic Journal of Behavioral Sciences* 16 (1994): 296–306.

Cole, Johnnetta, and Beverly Guy-Sheftall. *Gender Talk: The Struggle for Women's Equality in African American Communities*. New York: Striver's Row, 2003.

Collier-Thomas, Bettye, and James Turner. "Race, Class, and Color: The African American Discourse on Identity." *Journal of American Ethnic History* 14 (1994): 5–32.

Collins, Patricia Hill. *Black Feminist Thought*. New York: Routledge, 1991.

———. "Learning From the Outsider Within: The Sociological Significance of Black Feminist Thought." In *Beyond Methodology: Feminist Scholarship as Lived Research*, eds. Mary Margaret Fonow and Judith A. Cook. Bloomington: Indiana University Press, 1991.

———. *Fighting Words: Black Women and the Search for Justice*. Minneapolis: University of Minnesota Press, 1998.

———. *Black Sexual Politics: African Americans, Gender, and the New Racism*. New York: Routledge, 2004.

Cooper, Anna Julia. *A Voice From the South*. New York: Negro Universities Press, 1892.

Cortés, Carlos E. "Chicanas in Film: History of an Image." In *Latin Looks: Images of Latinas and Latinos in the U.S. Media*, ed. Clara E. Rodriguez. Boulder, CO: Westview Press, 1997.

Cortese, Anthony J. *Provocateur: Images of Women and Minorities in Advertising*. New York: Rowman & Littlefield, 1999.

Craig, Maxine Leeds. *Ain't I a Beauty Queen: Black Women, Beauty, and the Politics of Race*. New York: Oxford University Press, 2002.

Davila, Arlene M. *Latinos, Inc.* Berkeley: University of California Press, 2001.

Davis, Allison. *Deep South: A Social Anthropological Study of Caste and Class*. Chicago: University of Chicago Press, 1941.

Davis, Angela. *Women, Race, and Class*. New York: Vintage Books, 1981.

Davis, F. James. *Who Is Black? One Nation's Definition*. University Park: Pennsylvania State University Press, 1991.

Davis, Kathy. *Reshaping the Female Body*. New York: Routledge, 1995.

DeLeón, Arnoldo. *They Called Them Greasers: Anglo Attitudes Toward Mexicans in Texas, 1821-1900*. Austin: University of Texas Press, 1983.

DeVault, Marjorie. "Talking and Listening from Women's Standpoint: Feminist Strategies for Interviewing and Analysis." *Social Problems* 37, no. 1 (1990): 96–116.

Díaz del Castillo, Bernal. *The Conquest of New Spain*. Baltimore: Penguin Books, 1963.

Dill, Bonnie Thorton. "The Dialectics of Black Womanhood." In *Black Women in America*, eds. Micheline Malson, Elisabeth Mudimbe-Boyi, Jean O'Barr, and Mary Wyer. Chicago: University of Chicago Press, 1988.

Dominquez, Virginia R. *White By Definition: Social Classification in Creole Louisiana*. New Brunswick: Rutgers University Press, 1986.

Drake, St. Clair. *Black Folk Here and There, Volume One*. Los Angeles, UCLA CAAS: University of California Press, 1987.

Drake, St. Clair, and Horace R. Cayton. *Black Metropolis*. New York: Harcourt Brace, 1945.

Edwards, G. F. *The Negro Professional Class*. Glencoe, IL: The Free Press, 1959.

Edwards, Ozzie. "Skin Color as a Variable in Racial Attitudes of Black Urbanites." *Journal of Black Studies* 3 (1973): 473–483.

Elder, Glen. "Appearance and Education in Marriage Mobility." *American Sociological Review,* 34 (1969): 519–533.

Ernst, Klaus. "Racialism, Racialist Ideology, and Colonialism, Past and Present." In *Sociological Theories: Race and Colonialism*. United Kingdom: UNESCO, 1980.

Espino, Rodolfo, and Michael Franz. "Latino Phenotypic Discrimination Revisited: The Impact of Skin Color on Occupational Status." *Social Science Quarterly* 83, no. 2 (2002).

Etcoff, Nancy. *Survival of the Prettiest: The Science of Beauty*. New York: Anchor Books, 2000.

Fanon, Frantz. *Black Skin White Masks*. New York: Grove Weidenfeld, 1967.

Fischer, Claude, Michael Hout, Martín S. Jankowski, Samuel Lucas, Ann Swidler, and Kim Voss. *Inequality By Design: Cracking the Bell Curve Myth*. Princeton, NJ: Princeton University Press, 1996.

Fonow, Mary Margaret, and Judith A. Cook. *Beyond Methodology: Feminist Scholarship as Lived Research*. Bloomington: Indiana University Press, 1991.

Fonow, Mary Margaret, and Judith A. Cook. "Back to the Future: A Look at the Second Wave of Feminist Epistemology and Methodology." In *Beyond Methodology: Feminist Scholarship as Lived Research*, eds. Mary Margaret Fonow and Judith A. Cook. Bloomington: Indiana University Press, 1991.

Fraser, Suzanne. *Cosmetic Surgery, Gender, and Culture*. New York: Palgrave Macmillan, 2003.

Frazier, E. Franklin. *The Negro Family in the United States*. New York: The Dryden Press, 1951.

———. *Black Bourgeoisie*. New York: Collier Books, 1957.

Fredrickson, George. *White Supremacy*. Oxford: Oxford University Press, 1981.

Freedman, Rita. *Beauty Bound*. Lexington, MA: Lexington Books, 1986.

Freeman, Howard, David Armor, Michael Ross, and Thomas Pettigrew. "Color Gradation and Attitudes among Middle Income Negroes." *American Sociological Review* 31 (1966): 365–74.

Garcia, Alma. "The Development of Chicana Feminist Discourse, 1970-1980." *Gender & Society* 3, no. 2 (1989): 217–238.

Gatewood, Willard B. *Aristocrats of Color: The Black Elite 1880–1920*. Bloomington: Indiana University Press, 1990.

Giddings, Paula. *When and Where I Enter*. New York: Quill William Morrow, 1984.

Goering, Sara. "Conformity Through Cosmetic Surgery: The Medical Erasure of Race and Disability." In *Science and Other Cultures: Issues in Philosophies of Science and Technology*. New York: Routledge, 2003.

Gossett, Thomas F. *Race: The History of an Idea in America*. Dallas: Southern Methodist University Press, 1963.

Graham, Lawrence Otis. *Our Kind of People: Inside America's Black Upper Class*. New York: Perennial, 2000.

Guerrero, Andrés. *A Chicano Theology*. New York: Orbis Books, 1987.

Haiken, Elizabeth. *Venus Envy: A History of Cosmetic Surgery*. Baltimore: Johns Hopkins University Press, 1997.

Hall, Ronald. "'The Bleaching Syndrome': Implications of Light Skin for Hispanic American Assimilation." *Hispanic Journal of Behavioral Sciences* 16, no. 3 (1994): 307–14.

———. "The Bleaching Syndrome: African Americans' Response to Cultural Domination Vis-à-vis Skin Color." *Journal of Black Studies* 26, no. 2 (1995): 172–84.

———. "Dark Skin and the Cultural Ideal of Masculinity." *Journal of African American Men* 1, no. 3 (1995): 37–62.

Haller, Max. "Marriage, Women, and Social Stratification: A Theoretical Critique." *American Journal of Sociology* 86, no. 4 (1981): 766–95.

Harding, Sandra. *Feminism and Methodology*. Bloomington: Indiana University Press, 1987.

———. *Whose Science? Whose Knowledge? Thinking From Women's Lives*. Ithaca, NY: Cornell University Press, 1991.

Harris, Cheryl. "Whiteness as Property." In *Critical Race Theory*, eds. Kimberlé Crenshaw, Neil Gotanda, Gary Peller, and Kendall Thomas. New York: The New Press, 1995.

Hatfield, Elaine, and Susan Sprecher. *Mirror, Mirror: The Importance of Looks in Everyday Life*. Albany: State University of New York Press, 1986.

Hernton, Calvin. *Sex and Racism in America*. New York: Grove Press, 1965.

Herring, Cedric. "Skin Deep: Race and Complexion in the Color-Blind Era." In *Skin/Deep: How Race and Complexion Matter in the Color-Blind Era*, eds. Cedric Herring, Verna M. Keith, Hayward Derrick Horton. Urbana: University of Illinois Press, 2004.

Herrnstein, Richard J., and Charles Murray. *The Bell Curve: Intelligence and Class Structure in American Life*. New York: The Free Press, 1994.

Herron, Carolivia. *Nappy Hair*. New York: Dragonfly Books, 1998.

Hill, Mark E. "Color Differences in the Socioeconomic Status of African American Men: Results of a Longitudinal Study." *Social Forces* 78, no. 4 (2000): 1437–1460.

———. "Skin Color and the Perception of Attractiveness Among African Americans: Does Gender Make a Difference?" *Social Psychology Quarterly* 65, no. 1 (2002): 77–91.

Hoch, Paul. *White Hero Black Beast: Racism, Sexism and the Mask of Masculinity*. London: Pluto Press, 1979.

Hoefflin, Steven M. *Ethnic Rhinoplasty*. New York: Springer-Verlag, 1998.

Holland, Dorothy, and Margaret Eisenhart. *Educated in Romance*. Chicago: University of Chicago Press, 1990.

hooks, bell. *Ain't I a Woman? Black Women and Feminism*. Boston: South End Press, 1981.

———. *Happy to Be Nappy*. New York: Hyperion Press, 1999.

Horton, Hayward Derrick, and Lori Latrice Sykes. "Toward a Critical Demography of Neo-Mulattoes: Structural Change and Diversity Within the Black Population." In *Skin/Deep: How Race and Complexion Matter in the 'Color-Blind' Era*, eds. Cedric Herring, Verna M. Keith, and Hayward Derrick Horton. Urbana: University of Illinois Press, 2004.

Howard, Walter. *Lynchings: Extralegal Violence in Florida During the 1930s*. London: Associated Universities Press, 1995.

Hudson, J. Blaine. "The African Diaspora and the 'Black Atlantic': An African American Perspective." *Negro History Bulletin* 6, no. 4 (1997).

Hughes, Bradley, and Michael Hertel. "The Significance of Color Remains: A Study of Life

Chances, Mate Selection, and Ethnic Consciousness Among Black Americans." *Social Forces* 68, no. 4 (1990): 1105–20.

Hunter, Margaret. "Colorstruck: Skin Color Stratification in the Lives of African American Women." *Sociological Inquiry* 68, no. 4 (1998): 517–35.

———. "'If You're Light, You're Alright': Light Skin Color as Social Capital for Women of Color." *Gender & Society* 16, no. 2 (2002): 175–93.

Hunter, Margaret, and Kimberly D. Nettles, "What About the White Women?: Racial Politics in a Women's Studies Classroom." *Teaching Sociology* 27 (1999): 385–97.

Hunter, Margaret, Walter Allen, and Edward Telles. "The Significance of Skin Color among African Americans and Mexican Americans." *African American Research Perspectives* 7, no. 1 (2001): 173–84.

James, Angela. "Making Sense of Race and Racial Classification." *Race and Society* 4, no. 2. (2001): 235–47.

Jayaratne, Toby E., and Abigail J. Stewart. "Quantitative and Qualitative Methods in the Social Sciences: Current Feminist Issues and Practical Strategies." In *Beyond Methodology: Feminist Scholarship as Lived Research*, eds. Mary Margaret Fonow and Judith A. Cook. Bloomington: Indiana University Press, 1991.

Jewell, K. Sue. *From Mammy to Miss America and Beyond: Cultural Images and the Shaping of U.S. Social Policy*. New York: Routledge, 1993.

Jordan, Winthrop. *White Over Black*. Chapel Hill: University of North Carolina Press, 1968.

Kaw, Eugenia. "Medicalization of Racial Features: Asian American Women and Cosmetic Surgery." In *The Politics of Women's Bodies: Sexuality, Appearance, and Behavior*, ed. Rose Weitz. New York: Oxford University Press, 1998.

Keith, Verna, and Cedric Herring. 1991. "Skin Tone and Stratification in the Black Community." *American Journal of Sociology* 97, no. 3 (1991): 760–78.

King, Deborah. "Multiple Jeopardy, Multiple Consciousness: The Context of a Black Feminist Ideology." *Signs* 14, no. 1 (1988): 42–72.

Knight, Alan. "Racism, Revolution, and *Indigenismo*: Mexico, 1910-1940." In *The Idea of Race in Latin America*, ed. Richard Graham. Austin: University of Texas Press, 1990.

Lake, Obiagele. *Blue Veins and Kinky Hair: Naming and Color Consciousness in African America*. Westport, CT: Praeger, 2003.

Lakoff, Robin, and Racquel Scherr. *Face Value: The Politics of Beauty*. Boston: Routledge, 1984.

Leeds, Maxine. "Young African-American Women and the Language of Beauty." In *Ideals of Feminine Beauty: Philosophical, Social, and Cultural Dimensions*, ed. Karen Callaghan. London: Greenwood Press, 1994.

Leonardo, Zeus. "The Souls of White Folk: Critical Pedagogy, Whiteness Studies, and Globalization Discourse." *Race Ethnicity, and Education* 5, no. 1. (2002): 29–50.

Lewis, Amanda, Mark Chesler, and Tyrone Forman. "The Impact of 'Colorblind' Ideologies on Students of Color: Intergroup Relations at a Predominately White University." *Journal of Negro Education* 69, no. 1–2 (2000): 74–91.

Lewis, Diane K. "A Response to Inequality: Black Women, Racism, and Sexism." In *Black Women in America*, eds. Micheline R. Malson, Elisabeth Mudimbe-Boyi, Jean F. O'Barr, and Mary Wyer. Chicago: University of Chicago Press, 1988.

Lopez, David. *Language Maintenance and Shift in the U.S. Today: The Basic Patterns and Their Implications*. Los Alamitos, CA: National Center for Bilingual Research, 1982.

Lorde, Audre. *Sister Outsider*. New York: Crossing Press, 1984.

Los Angeles County Museum of Art, *Inventing Race: Casta Painting and Eighteenth-Century Mexico*. Los Angeles: LACMA, 2004.

Luciano, Lynne. *Looking Good: Male Body Image in Modern America*. New York: Hill and Wang Publishers, 2001.

Lux, Guillermo and Maurilio Vigil. "Return to Aztlán: The Chicano Rediscovers His Indian Past." In *Aztlán: Essays on the Chicano Homeland*, eds. Rudolfo Anaya and Francisco Lomelí. Albuquerque: University of New Mexico Press, 1989.

Martinez, George. "Mexican Americans and Whiteness." In *Critical White Studies*, eds. Richard Delgado and Jean Stefancic. Philadelphia: Temple University Press, 1997.

Memmi, Albert. *The Colonizer and the Colonized*. Boston: Beacon Press, 1965.

Mies, Maria. "Towards a Methodology for Feminist Research." In *Theories of Women's Studies*, eds. G. Bowles and R. Klein. Boston: Routledge, 1983.

Montalvo, F. *Skin Color and Latinos: The Origins and Contemporary Patterns of Ethnoracial Ambiguity Among Mexican Americans and Puerto Ricans* (monograph). San Antonio, TX: Our Lady of the Lake University, 1987.

Montiel, Miguel. "The Social Science Myth of the Mexican American Family." *El Grito*, 3 (1970): 56–63.

Moore, Joan, and Harry Pachon. *Hispanics in the United States*. Englewood Cliffs, NJ: Prentice Hall, 1985.

Moraga, Cherríe. "La Güera." In *This Bridge Called My Back: Radical Writings by Women of Color*, eds. Gloria Anzaldúa and Cherríe Moraga. New York: Kitchen Table Press, 1983.

Morgan, Kathryn Pauly. "Women and the Knife: Cosmetic Surgery and the Colonization of Women's Bodies." In *The Politics of Women's Bodies: Sexuality, Appearance, and Behavior*, ed. Rose Weitz. New York: Oxford University Press, 1998.

Mörner, Magnus. *Race Mixture in the History of Latin America*. Boston: Little, Brown, 1967.

Morrison, Toni. *Playing in the Dark: Whiteness and the Literary Imagination*. New York: Vintage Books, 1992.

Mullings, Leith. "Images, Ideology, and Women of Color." In *Women of Color in U.S. Society*, eds. Maxine Baca Zinn and Bonnie Thornton Dill. Philadelphia: Temple University Press, 1994.

Mullins, Elizabeth, and Paul Sites. "The Origins of Contemporary Eminent Black Americans: A Three Generation Analysis of Social Origin." *American Sociological Review* 49 (1984): 672–85.

Murguia, Edward, and Edward Telles. "Phenotype and Schooling among Mexican Americans." *Sociology of Education* 69 (1996): 276–89.

Nagel, Joane. *Race, Ethnicity, and Sexuality: Intimate Intersections and Forbidden Frontiers*. New York: Oxford University Press, 2003.

National Association for the Advancement of Colored People. *Thirty Years of Lynching in the U.S. 1889–1918*. New York: Negro Universities Press, 1969.

Oakley, Ann. "Interviewing Women: A Contradiction in Terms." In *Doing Feminist Research*, ed. Helen Roberts. London: Routledge, 1981.

Okazawa-Rey, Margo, Tracy Robinson, and Janie V. Ward. "Black Women and the Politics of Skin Color and Hair." *Women's Studies Quarterly* 14, nos. 1, 2 (1986).

Omi, Michael, and Howard Winant. *Racial Formation in the United States*. New York: Routledge, 1994.

Orozco, Cynthia. " Sexism in Chicano Studies and the Community." In *Chicana Voices: Intersections of Class, Race, and Gender*, eds. Teresa Córdova, Norma Cantú, Gilberto Cardenas, Juan García, and Christine Sierra. Albuquerque: University of New Mexico Press, 1990.

Ortiz, Vilma. "Women of Color: A Demographic Overview." In *Women of Color in U.S. Society*, eds. Maxine Baca Zinn and Bonnie Thornton Dill. Philadelphia: Temple University Press, 1994.

———. "The Mexican-Origin Population: Permanent Working Class or Emerging Middle Class?" In *Ethnic Los Angeles*, eds. Roger Waldinger and Mehdi Bozorgmehr. New York: Russell Sage Foundation, 1996.

Ortiz, Vilma, and Carlos Arce. "Language Orientation and Mental Health Status Among Persons of Mexican Descent." *Hispanic Journal of Behavioral Sciences* 6 (1984): 127–43.

Penha-Lopes, Vânia. "Race South of the Equator: Reexamining the Intersection of Color and Class in Brazil." In *Skin/Deep: How Race and Complexion Matter in the 'Color-Blind' Era*, eds. Cedric Herring, Verna M. Keith, and Hayward Derrick Horton. Urbana: University of Illinois Press, 2004.

Pérez, Emma. "Speaking from the Margin: Uninvited Discourse on Sexuality and Power." In *Building With Our Hands: New Directions in Chicana Studies*, eds. Adela de la Torre and Beatríz Pesquera. Berkeley: University of California Press, 1993.

Ramírez, Oscar M. "Facial Plastic Surgery in the Hispano-American Patient." In *Ethnic Considerations in Facial Aethetic Surgery*, ed. W. Earle Matory Jr. Philadelphia: Lippincott-Raven Publishers, 1998.

Ransford, H. E. "Skin Color, Life Chances, and Anti-White Attitude." *Social Problems* 18 (1970): 164–78.

Relethford, J., P. Stern, S.P. Catskill, and H.P. Hazuda. "Social Class, Admixture, and Skin Color Variation in Mexican Americans and Anglo Americans Living in San Antonio, Texas." *American Journal of Physical Anthropology* 61 (1983): 97–102.

Reuter, E. B. *The Mulatto in the United States.* New York: Negro University Press, 1918.

Riessman, Catherine Kohler. "When Gender is Not Enough: Women Interviewing Women" *Gender and Society* 1, no. 2 (1987): 172–207.

Rivera, Jenny. "Domestic Violence Against Latinas by Latino Males: An Analysis of Race, National Origin, and Gender Differentials." In *Critical Race Feminism*, ed. Adrien Katherine Wing. New York: New York University Press, 1997.

Roberts, Dorothy. *Killing the Black Body.* New York: Pantheon Books, 1997.

Robinson, Tracy L., and Janie V. Ward. "African American Adolescents and Skin Color." *Journal of Black Psychology* 21, no. 3 (1995): 256–74.

Rockquemore, Kerry Ann. "Between Black and White: Exploring the "Biracial" Experience." *Race and Society* 1, no. 2, (1998): 202.

Rooks, Noliwe M. *Hair Raising: Beauty, Culture, and African American Women.* New Brunswick: Rutgers University Press, 1996.

Root, Maria P. P. "Mixed Race Women." In *Race Sex: Their Sameness, Difference, and Interplay*, ed. Naomi Zack. New York: Routledge, 1997.

Ruiz, Vicki. *From Out of the Shadows: Mexican Women in Twentieth Century America.* New York: Oxford University Press, 1998.

Russell, Kathy, Midge Wilson, and Ronald Hall. *The Color Complex.* New York: Doubleday, 1992.

Scales-Trent, Judy. *Notes of a White Black Woman: Race, Color, and Community.* University Park: Pennsylvania State University Press, 1995.

Segura, Denise, and Beatriz M. Pesquera. "Beyond Indifference and Antipathy: The Chicana Movement and Chicana Feminist Discourse." *Aztlan* 19, no. 2 (1988): 69–92.

Seltzer, Richard, and Robert C. Smith. "Color Differences in the Afro-American Community and the Differences They Make." *Journal of Black Studies* 21, no. 3 (1991): 279–86.

Smith, Dorothy. "Women's Perspective as Radical Critique of Sociology." In *Feminism and Methodology*, ed. Sandra Harding. Bloomington: Indiana University Press, 1987.

Stanley, Liz and Sue Wise. *Breaking Out: Feminist Consciousness and Feminist Research.* Boston: Routledge, 1983.

Stevenson, Brenda. *Life in Black and White: Family and Community in the Slave South.* New York: Oxford University Press, 1996.

Sullivan, Deborah A. *Cosmetic Surgery: The Cutting Edge of Commercial Medicine in America.* New Brunswick: Rutgers University Press, 2001.

Telles, Edward, and Edward Murguia. "Phenotypic Discrimination and Income Differences among Mexican Americans." *Social Science Quarterly* 71, no. 4 (1990): 682–96.

Thompson, Maxine S., and Verna Keith. "The Blacker the Berry: Gender, Skin Tone, Self-Esteem, and Self-Efficacy." *Gender & Society* 15, no. 3 (2001): 336–57.

Tucker, M. Belinda, and Claudia Mitchell-Kernan. "Psychological Well-Being and Perceived Marital Opportunity Among Single African American, Latina, and White Women." *Journal of Comparative Family Studies* 29, no. 1 (1998): 57–72.

Udry, Richard, Karl Baumann, and Charles Chase. "Skin Color, Status, and Mate Selection." *American Journal of Sociology* 76, no. 4 (1971): 722–33.

Vasconcelos, José. *La Raza Cósmica, Misión de la Raza Iberoamericana.* Paris: Agencia Mundial de Librería, 1925.

Wallace, Michelle. "Anger in Isolation: A Black Feminist's Search for Sisterhood." In *Words of Fire: An Anthology of African American Feminist Thought*, ed. Beverly Guy-Sheftall. New York: The New Press, 1995.

Waters, Mary. *Ethnic Options: Choosing Identities in America.* Berkeley: University of California Press, 1990.

Webster, Murray Jr., and James Driskell Jr. "Beauty as Status." *American Journal of Sociology* 89, no. 1 (1983): 140–65.

Williamson, Joel. *New People: Miscegenation and Mulattos in the United States.* Baton Rouge: Louisiana University Press, 1995.

Wolf, Naomi. *The Beauty Myth: How Images of Beauty are Used Against* Women. New York: Doubleday Books, 1991.

Zavella, Patricia. "Reflections on Diversity Among Chicanas." In *Challenging Fronteras: Structuring Latina and Latino Lives in the U.S.*, eds. Mary Romero, Pierrette Hondagneu-Sotelo, and Vilma Ortiz. New York: Routledge, 1997.

Zinn, Maxine Baca. "Gender and Ethnic Identity Among Chicanos." *Frontiers* 5, no. 2 (1980): 18–24.

Zinn, Maxine Baca, and Bonnie Thornton Dill. "Theorizing Difference from Multiracial Feminism." *Feminist Studies* 22, no. 2 (1996): 321–31.

# INDEX